Sufi Mysticism and Jungian Psychology

In a time of global uncertainty and spiritual searching, *Sufi Mysticism and Jungian Psychology: Individuation, Self-realization, Higher Consciousness* brings two visionary thinkers into dialogue to explore the inner journey of transformation that connects East and West, psyche and soul.

This book offers a comparative exploration of Carl Gustav Jung's analytical psychology and Sufi mysticism as articulated by Hazrat Inayat Khan, illuminating how each tradition understands the transformation of consciousness. Through themes such as active imagination, the alchemical process of inner integration, the purification of the heart, music as a metaphysical force, and realization of the self through love and guidance, the book traces a shared path toward wholeness. In a world marked by fragmentation and existential disorientation, it reveals how these two voices – one psychological, the other spiritual – speak to the longing for meaning, coherence, and connection with higher dimensions of consciousness.

What sets this book apart is its original dialogical approach, culminating in an imagined encounter between Carl Jung and Inayat Khan, set in a historic intellectual soirée. While written in an accessible and engaging style, the book is grounded in careful research, drawing on primary sources, archival material, and recent scholarship in psychology, mysticism, and religious studies. It opens up new perspectives on the relationship between East and West, science and spirituality, offering both depth and clarity for scholarly and general readers drawn to inner transformation and cultural dialogue.

Karin Jironet, Ph.D., is a Sufi Murshida, Jungian psychoanalyst, and internationally published author whose work integrates the disciplines of mysticism and analytical psychology. Working globally, she guides individuals and organizations in the articulation of consciousness and the cultivation of purposeful presence. Her writing explores the transformative potential of breath, imagination, and love as doorways to individuation, self-realization, and collective awakening. *Sufi Mysticism and Jungian Psychology* reflects a lifelong devotion to the inner path and its relevance in a time of profound cultural and spiritual transition.

"Carl Jung and Inayat Khan apparently never met, but there are remarkable convergences and complementarities between their bodies of work. In this volume, the minds of these two great thinkers of the early twentieth century are brought into dynamic dialogue. The result is a delightful and inspiring exploration of the generative nexus where psychology and mysticism intersect."

Pir Zia Inayat Khan, *author of* Tears from the Mother of the Sun

"*Sufi Mysticism and Jungian Psychology* is a valuable contribution to the ongoing dialogue between Jungian psychology and the world's spiritual traditions, in this case Sufism. Karin Jironet brings many years of study and experience to this work. Her sterling qualifications should give confidence to readers that they are in the sure hands of a most competent interpreter and guide. In these pages, the sea of deep scholarship meets the sea of elevated inspiration. The combination is fresh and exhilarating."

Murray Stein, Ph.D., *author of* Jung's Map of the Soul

"This book is a confluence of two sacred streams. Here we experience the meeting of spiritual and psychological. It is a meeting of the East and the West and a meeting of science and wisdom. In a world of confusion and conflicts such synthesis is urgently needed. Karin Jironet has masterfully woven together these two great traditions represented by Carl Jung and Hazrat Inayat Khan, to help readers to understand and embrace a new worldview rooted in harmony and love. Congratulations to Karin Jironet for writing this timely and inspiring book. May it help to bring the birth of a new consciousness."

Satish Kumar, *Editor Emeritus*, Resurgence & Ecologist

"A lifetime of research and practice culminates in this passionate and insightful new study by psychoanalyst and religious scholar Karin Jironet, who creates a compelling cross-cultural dialogue between Carl Gustav Jung and Hazrat Inayat Khan on the nature of self and consciousness against the backdrop of a rapidly changing world."

Prof. Dr. Gerard Wiegers, *History and Comparative Study of Religions; Chair Religious Studies and History of Hermetic Philosophy, University of Amsterdam*

"How does psychosocial development evolve, and how is consciousness formed? The author explores these questions by comparing the Sufi mysticism of Hazrat Inayat Khan with the psychoanalysis of Carl Gustav Jung. In both traditions, lived experience is central. These experiences reflect the historical moment in which people live. As such, the book offers profound insight into individuation and self-realization and also into the evolution of the spirit of the age. Both thinkers lived in a time of unstable structures that called for renewal from within. For this reason, the book is particularly relevant for our own time."

Dr. G.P.P. van Tillo, *Professor Emeritus of the Sociology of Religion, University of Amsterdam*

"C.G. Jung's encounter in the Red Book with Izdubar, the 'man from the East,' 'he, from the light; I, from the darkness,' was fateful for him. Karin Jironet's book sheds light on the encounter between East and West by comparing Inayat Khan's Sufism with Jung's Analytical Psychology. Both faced the challenge of reconciling Eastern spiritual traditions with Western rationalism, recognizing that the collapse of outer structures in our world calls for an *inner renewal*. A valuable contribution to the dialogue!"

Dr. Andreas Schweizer, *Past President of the Psychology Club, Zurich*

"Jung only had a limited connection with Sufism, and none with Hazrat Inayat Khan. Jironet's previous work and now this book, bring the parallels between them alive, adding a greater dimension to the concept of individuation and its goal of the realization of the Self, a tradition refined in Sufism over 1,300 years that Hazrat Inayat Khan brought to the West."

Leslie Stein, *Jungian Analyst, The University of Sydney*

"Karin Jironet has written a powerful new book that will deeply impact people who are on a quest for deeper meaning in their lives. By creating an imaginary dialogue between Carl Jung and Hazrat Inayat Khan, two of the finest minds of our world, she has enabled us to source rich insights for our lives. Carl Jung's work helps us to appreciate what truly matters to us and make sense of all rituals, myths, stories that have shaped us.

Inayat Khan helps us to prepare for the inner journey beyond ego-centric desires and the limitations of senses, mind, and intellect to the Silence within the consciousness that is all pervading in the universe. If Jung is helping us to interpret our dreams and delve into the unconscious, Inayat Khan is taking us on a journey of self-realization and appreciating the role of divine music that nourishes our soul. Karin writes with freedom and creativity, and her work will set us on a path to source deep inspiration that will make us all 'rise' in love for serving the well-being of all by discovering our paths of deep meaning, peace and harmony."

Anil Sachdev, *Founder and Chairman of the School of Inspired Leadership, New Delhi*

Sufi Mysticism and Jungian Psychology

Individuation, Self-realization, Higher Consciousness

Karin Jironet

Routledge
Taylor & Francis Group

LONDON AND NEW YORK

Designed cover image: Getty Images. *The Place Where Two Seas Meet*, is an original design by Christina Schumacher of RocktheNet.

First published 2026
by Routledge
4 Park Square, Milton Park, Abingdon, Oxon OX14 4RN

and by Routledge
605 Third Avenue, New York, NY 10158

Routledge is an imprint of the Taylor & Francis Group, an informa business

For Product Safety Concerns and Information please contact our EU representative GPSR@taylorandfrancis.com. Taylor & Francis Verlag GmbH, Kaufingerstraße 24, 80331 München, Germany.

British Library Cataloguing-in-Publication Data
A catalogue record for this book is available from the British Library

ISBN: 978-1-032-55592-8 (hbk)
ISBN: 978-1-032-55591-1 (pbk)
ISBN: 978-1-003-43133-6 (ebk)

DOI: 10.4324/9781003431336

Typeset in Times New Roman
by Apex CoVantage, LLC

For Harry Starren, companion in the real, the silent, and the becoming.

Contents

Acknowledgments[1]

Carl Gustav Jung   Hazrat Inayat Khan

Karimbakhsh Witteveen

Murray Stein   Pir Zia Inayat Khan

Isa Haberer

Mureeds

Analysands

Filip Jironet   Disa Jironet

Harry Starren

Note

1 In the spirit of this work, I have chosen to acknowledge certain individuals simply by name. Each offered something essential, be it insight, companionship, questions, or presence – often without asking and always beyond measure. Gratitude is not always best explained.

Contents

Acknowledgments[1]

Carl Gustav Jung   Hazrat Inayat Khan

Karimbakhsh Witteveen

Murray Stein   Pir Zia Inayat Khan

Isa Haberer

Mureeds

Analysands

Filip Jironet   Disa Jironet

Harry Starren

Note

1 In the spirit of this work, I have chosen to acknowledge certain individuals simply by name. Each offered something essential, be it insight, companionship, questions, or presence – often without asking and always beyond measure. Gratitude is not always best explained.

Note on Sources

Throughout this book, I have quoted from the published writings of Hazrat Inayat Khan and C. G. Jung. In both cases, care has been taken to use brief, clearly attributed passages that serve a reflective and scholarly purpose.

Quotations from *The Sufi Message of Hazrat Inayat Khan* refer to the 1988 fourteen-volume edition published by Motilal Banarsidass (Delhi), a comprehensive and widely referenced source. Identical versions of these texts are also freely accessible through the Hazrat Inayat Khan Study Database, an open public archive: www.hazrat-inayat-khan.org.

Citations from Jung's *Red Book* are drawn from *The Red Book: Liber Novus (Reader's Edition)*, edited by Sonu Shamdasani (W. W. Norton, 2009). This edition is also available through academic libraries and public archives. The passages selected reflect themes central to Jung's visionary psychology and resonate with the mystical path explored here.

All quotations are used under fair use for purposes of analysis, interpretation, and study. Full bibliographic details appear in the reference section.

Foreword by Shaikh al-Mashaik Mahmood Khan[1]

For a long time now, it has been recognized that Hazrat Inayat Khan's "Indian" Sufism is a treasure trove awaiting exploration by a multitude of scholarly disciplines.

Hazrat himself was convinced that the difference between science and mysticism was a temporary one, and that both approaches to understanding and awareness would increasingly converge and ultimately be bridged.

In his most personal field of Indian classical music, in its twofold appearance of "Hindustani" and "Carnatic" (Northern and Southern styles), Hazrat moved increasingly toward philosophical comprehension through his teachings on tone, sound, vibration, and aesthetic contemplation as anticipations of mystical meditation.

These notions have become familiar among musicians and musicological specialists rather than among those who regard themselves as followers or disciples of his Sufism. But also in epistemology, Inayat Khan proved a veritable pioneer. He insisted that in matters not only of art and spirituality but also of intellectual concept and research, the primary drive was intuitive rather than purely rational. One's entry into a particular field of study is often driven by subjective affinity. The "imagining of thought" is now a generally accepted view. A century ago, the contrast between the heart's intuitive perceptions and the intellectual achievements of discursive knowledge still appeared in stark dualism. Poetic and philosophical imagination have always been twins.

It is worth, in this context, looking at Hazrat Inayat Khan's psychology. In his approach, the human being is constituted threefold: body, psyche, and soul. The second, psychological level consists of mind and heart – intellect and intuition. And in an oft-repeated Inayatian phrase: "The mind is the surface of the heart, the heart is the depth of the mind."

Rather than the physical form, it is the unseen characteristics of mind and heart that determine the quality of personality. And yet it is the third and highest level – the soul – that, while intangible and unperceivable unless consciously discovered, ultimately may attune and determine the quality of the heart and mind, and thus of personality in its entirety.

Hazrat Inayat Khan's psychology is, of course, not modern clinical psychology, but the traditional philosophical kind. "Psychology," he writes, "is learned by the

analysis and synthesis of all that we can feel in human nature and in our character . . . it is learned by thinking" – by discursive and contemplative reflection.

One of Hazrat's key phrases is "when one observes life keenly," and contemporary memories recall his extraordinary powers of observation and perception.
Psychology, in his system, is part of the triad: Philosophy, Psychology, Mysticism.

This leads us directly to the extraordinarily rich content of the present book.

In this remarkable study, Dr. Karin Jironet combines the celebrated Dr. C. G.
Jung's empirical and conceptual psychology with the contemplative, aesthetic, and
meditative-mystical Sufism of Hazrat Inayat Khan in a way that amounts to a novel
joint understanding of these two giants of the spirit. And this is presented not just as
a qualified observer, but as an active participant. Few studies today could be more
relevant, and even fewer scholars have the competence and initiative to undertake
such a massive and meaningful task.

I have had the privilege of knowing Dr. Karin Jironet since her Amsterdam
promovenda days, during which her dedication to confronting and combining the
intellectual and spiritual values of human life blossomed into increasing fullness,
practiced in a life enriched with psychological expertise and incisive Sufi insight.
For over two decades, she has maintained a wide psychoanalytic practice, integrating clinical training with her spiritual lineage. Her grounding includes formative
study in Zürich, as well as long-standing commitment to embodied psychological
work and Sufi contemplation. Dr. Carl Gustav Jung has had many competent suc-
cessors. Hazrat Inayat Khan's Indian Sufism has found an altogether exceptional
representative and spokesman in his grandson Pir Zia Inayat Khan. Yet, apart from
such specialists, the popularity of both Jung's and Inayat Khan's teachings sometimes risks circling in self-contained repetition. Dr. Jironet's work breaks through
these cycles. She demonstrates how both men, in distinct ways, open up a totality
of insights enriching our entire conception of the human spirit – however defined.

This represents a renewal of insight in a field paradoxically grown barren
through both professional overgrowth and popular neglect.

This is not the first time Dr. Jironet has published groundbreaking work. Her
2009 *Sufism into the West: Life and Leadership of Hazrat Inayat Khan's Brothers
1927–1967* is as delightful as it is insightful. In well-written pages, she brings to
life not only their actions and attitudes but also the wit and elegance that permeate
Hazrat Inayat Khan's own writings. Her ability to round off her observations with
clarity and force is striking.

These qualities have deepened in the present book, a truly enriching contribution. Each chapter is a genuine surprise. Let me mention two that stood out to me.

Chapter 6 offers a masterful summary of Hazrat Inayat Khan's views and
teachings. It should be in the hands of every serious student of his Indian Sufism.
And Chapter 7, "An Envisioned Dialogue: Where the Two Seas Meet," may be
regarded as the centerpiece. The imagined dialogue between Jung and Inayat Khan,
accompanied by surprising guests, recalls the spirit of Plato's dialogues: evocative,
poetic, and deeply illuminating. It is accomplished in a way that modern readers
will find both inspiring and delightfully light in tone. Dr. Jironet shows herself a

true disciple of Hazrat Inayat Khan and of Carl Gustav Jung, uniting conceptual depth with lightness of touch and a qualifying sense of humor, whether perceived or subtly implicit.

In reviewing this fascinating book, which opens new vistas of joint psychological and spiritual awareness, Dr. Jironet is truly to be congratulated.

– Shaikh Mahmood

Note

1 Shaikh al-Mashaik Mahmood Khan, born 1927, through his father, is directly related to Hazrat Inayat Khan and has long served as a respected guide in his lineage. A man of deep learning and modest bearing, he brings personal insight and historical depth to this foreword.

Chapter 1

The Call for Consciousness
Bridging East and West

This book is the culmination of a lifelong journey – a quest to understand the evolution of consciousness through two seemingly distant yet profoundly resonant pathways: Carl Gustav Jung's analytical psychology and Hazrat Inayat Khan's Sufism. Their teachings, grounded in distinct traditions, converge in their shared focus on self-realization and individuation as transformative processes that awaken the soul and integrate the psyche.

My first encounter with Jung's work was during my Ph.D. research on Hazrat Inayat Khan and the Sufi Movement.[1] Immersed in the study of Inayat Khan's teachings of love, harmony, beauty, and unity, I became acutely aware of a puzzling dichotomy: while his message inspired unity, the community itself was often marked by interpersonal conflicts and power struggles. This paradox led me to Jung's concept of the shadow, both personal and collective, as a lens to understand these dynamics. It revealed that such tensions, far from being mere obstacles, were invitations for growth, integration, and the deepening of wholeness. These insights marked the beginning of my integration of Jung's psychology with Sufi mysticism.[2]

My personal journey into spirituality and consciousness began long before my academic pursuits. As a young seeker, I explored practices ranging from Transcendental Meditation to Zen, eventually finding my spiritual home in Hazrat Inayat Khan's Sufism. A transformative moment came during my first visit to the Sufi Summer School in Katwijk, where I met Johannes Karimbakhsh Witteveen, who became my spiritual guide for over 26 years. My lived experience, combined with my training as a Jungian psychoanalyst, has profoundly shaped my understanding of the interplay between spirituality, psychology, and the evolution of consciousness.

At its heart, the book asks: What is the nature of consciousness, and how do Jung's analytical psychology and Inayat Khan's Sufism guide us toward its realization? These two paths, though distinct, illuminate complementary aspects of the human journey: the alchemical transformation of the psyche and the soulful unfolding of the heart. Together, they offer a framework for navigating the complexities of modern life, reconnecting with the divine, and awakening to a higher state of being.

DOI: 10.4324/9781003431336-1

Structure of the Book

The content is structured in five interconnected sections and one epilogue:

1. Introduction. We begin by broadly reflecting on the nature of mystical and numinous experiences, and how such experiences may prompt the widening of consciousness. This includes sensory experiences and phenomenological pathways to understanding the experiential journey of individuation and self-realization, themes central to the book.
2. Historical Contexts and Core Concepts. The second part explores the specific historical roots, biographical contexts, and relevant core concepts of Carl Jung's analytical psychology and Hazrat Inayat Khan's Sufism.
3. An Envisioned Dialogue, Where the Two Seas Meet. The third section features an imagined dialogue between the two, engaging with central themes drawn from their teachings and life experiences. This dynamic exchange invites readers to explore Jung's and Inayat Khan's ideas in a creative, reflective, and participatory way.
4. Convergence and Divergence at the Suez Delta. The chapter delves into the shared and differing perspectives of Jung and Inayat Khan, illuminating how their paths intersect and diverge. It reflects on the profound yet distinct ways they approach self-realization, individuation, and the transformation of consciousness.
5. The Call for Consciousness. The final section reflects on how their historical contexts bear striking similarities to today's challenges. It examines the nature of consciousness and its development through their lenses, emphasizing the timeless relevance of their insights for personal and collective transformation.
6. Epilogue. I conclude with my personal reflections in the epilogue, where I step away from analysis to share something more intimate. Reflecting on what the journey has meant for me, I explore how the themes of self-realization, individuation, and consciousness have shaped my understanding and my life. I invite the reader to consider their own path – where insights gleaned from Jung, Inayat Khan, and the broader human experience may resonate most deeply in their personal search for meaning.

More than an intellectual exercise, the book is an invitation to a deeply personal exploration. It seeks to inspire readers to listen to the call of consciousness, to awaken to their true nature, and to contribute to the collective journey toward a more harmonious and integrated world.

Notes

1 Karin Jironet, *The Image of Spiritual Liberty in the Sufi Movement Following Hazrat Inayat Khan* (Leuven: Peeters Publishers, 2002).
2 Karin Jironet, *Sufi Mysticism into the West: Life and Leadership of Hazrat Inayat Khan's Brothers 1927–1967 (New Religious Identities in the Western World)* (Peeters, 2009).

Chapter 2

A Phenomenological Approach to Analytical Psychology and Sufi Mysticism

Carl Gustav Jung (1875–1961) and Hazrat Inayat Khan (1882–1927) were very different men. Jung, the analytical psychologist, born in Swiss Kesswil into a Protestant family, and Inayat Khan, the Sufi sage, born in south-central India in Baroda into a Muslim family centered around music and may even seem incomparable giants.

Yet, their lives as well as their work show profound insights into human life and psychological and psychospiritual development. For one, although both Inayat Khan[1] and Jung were deeply endowed, trained, and proficient teachers in their respective traditions, Sufi mysticism and psychoanalysis, the teachings they taught drew on their direct personal experiences from the inner life which largely informed the meaning of their work.

Their direct personal experiences translate into enormous bodies of written sources that transcend their respective traditions and yield personal accounts offering glimpses into how consciousness evolves in their cases and potentially in general.

Despite their differing cultural and intellectual backgrounds, Hazrat Inayat Khan's teachings on *self-realization* and Carl Gustav Jung's concept of *individuation* share several essential themes and processes. To illustrate, individuation, according to Jung, is the individual's journey toward the self, the center of the person, through a process of divesting the false self, the *persona*, and forming a vital relationship with the unconscious, personal and collective, and so realize wholeness. Self-realization in Inayat Khan's Sufism is the journey of the Soul from its source through life and back. The journey, marked by awakening, follows a process of shedding and liberation from the false self, the *nafs*, and realization of God's divine nature, *fana'*.

Mysticism, numinous, and mystical experiences are not just shared themes. They are fundamental to Jung and Inayat Khan as essential processes that reflect a deeper engagement with the divine. Mystical and numinous experiences are the driving forces in individuation and self-realization. And everyone, now as then, has access to such experiences throughout life.

DOI: 10.4324/9781003431336-2

Mysticism and Mystical Experiences

Have you ever sensed that you were observed from afar and turned around to look? Finding yourself alone in the park, yet with an intense feeling of a being nearby? Or, has your eye caught the sight of a bird close to you while feeling a very real sense of communion with that bird? "Presence" and "unity of existence" are two common mystical experiences. And if you have spontaneously had such experiences, how did you become aware of it and its impact on your consciousness?

A mystical experience, however big or small, has a *noetic* quality, meaning that the experience to some extent transforms the person's consciousness through that direct encountering with ultimate reality, which is felt to be "more real than real."

Defining mystical experiences obviously forms a dilemma because those with such direct experience cannot formulate the nature of the same even if they wanted to, which most often is not the case, because definition would objectify the mystical and deprive the person of the real experience. Let alone, it would collapse the energetic insight and awareness and its ensuing wish for expression, for creativity.

Mystical experiences can be likened to numinous experiences. Rudolf Otto, the early 20th-century German theologian who first coined the term, described a numinous experience as a moment of being directly face to face with the holy, in the presence of the holy, or even united with what is experienced as undeniably holy. Such a moment, Otto says, has the quality of *mysterium tremendum et fascinans*: the mystery before which we simultaneously tremble and are fascinated. Otto, influenced not only by his teacher, the German philosopher and theologian Friedrich Schleiermacher, but by William James and his empirical work on religious experiences,

> James's emphasis on the *individual's* inner experience as central to religious understanding led Otto to focus on the affective, emotional and awe-inducing dimensions of encountering numinous experiences.

James's description of the "more real than real" quality that mystical experiences hold for those who have them suggest an encounter with a reality that transcends ordinary life and cannot be fully articulated, only directly felt. In *Das Heilige* (1917) (transl. *The Idea of the Holy*) Otto emphasizes the irrational character of the experience of such overwhelming glory of the holy, of God, during which rational mind and intellectual processes are temporarily suspended.[2]

Let us now take a closer look at how mysticism and mystical experiences have been studied, documented, and researched in the light of William James's fundamental contribution to the field – a universalist approach defining four marks of mysticism being ineffability, noetic quality, transiency, and passivity, all of which will inform our further in-depth comprehension of the teachings of Hazrat Inayat Khan and Carl Gustav Jung.

William James and Mystical Experience

William James's (1842–1910) *The Varieties of Religious Experience: A Study in Human Nature* (1902) remains a cornerstone in the study of mystical and religious experiences.[3] James, the renowned Harvard psychologist and philosopher, explored the personal, often private nature of such experiences while identifying commonalities across religious traditions. His work was instigated by an invitation to deliver the Gifford Lectures on natural religion at the University of Edinburgh.

James's own life was marked by health issues, beginning in childhood and culminating in a severe heart condition following a strenuous vacation in 1898. This period of physical distress resulted in a prolonged sabbatical in Europe, during which he prepared the Gifford Lectures. His lectures were notable for their rich descriptions and the pairing of concrete examples with insightful interpretation. James argued that, although mystical experiences are individually unique, they often point to a universal source of consciousness that may become accessible, for example, in times of existential crisis, revealing an innate, transcendent meaning.

To the universal categories he describes belong, in addition to the aforementioned *noetic* quality and *ineffability*, also *transience* and *passivity*. Transiency refers to these experiences' short-lived nature, lasting from one minute to up to an hour or two only. Passivity reflects the sense that mystical experiences are beyond the individual's normal control and seem to come from an external source, be it divine, cosmic, or otherwise. So, although mystical states may be facilitated, for instance, by concentration, attention, practices such as yoga, or in other ways, once the state of consciousness is awakened the person often feels a sense of surrender and as though they are being acted upon by an external force or presence.

One compelling example James presents is from Leo Tolstoy's personal search for meaning, which the Russian writer describes in *My Confession* (1882)[4] and *The Kingdom of God is Within You* (1894).[5] At around the age of 50, Tolstoy recounts his moments of profound perplexity and what he calls an "arrest," where the meaning of life itself seemed to disappear:

> Things were meaningless whose meaning had always been self-evident. The questions 'Why?' and 'What next?' began to beset me more and more frequently . . .
> I felt that something had broken within me on which my life had always rested, that I had nothing left to hold on to, and that morally my life had stopped.

Despite having all the outward signs of happiness – a loving family, material wealth, and professional success – Tolstoy was consumed by despair, having become disillusioned with the banality of life.

James reflects on Tolstoy's existential crisis, noting how profoundly disconnected traditional sources of comfort and optimism seemed in the face of such spiritual desolation. He writes: "Here is the real core of the religious problem: Help! Help! No prophet can claim to bring a final message unless he says things that will have a sound of reality in the ears of victims such as these."

James further shows how Tolstoy's deepening disenchantment eventually gave way to a spiritual awakening, an exaltation that emerged not through intellectual effort or external authority but organically, over time, infused by a series of numinous experiences. Tolstoy realized that true happiness lies in the infinite – a realm beyond the reach of rational thought. James likens this transformation to the passion of love, where a shift in consciousness occurs spontaneously: "If it comes, it comes, and no process of reasoning can force it."

Tolstoy's journey illustrates the inductive nature of numinous and mystical experiences – rooted in personal crisis and often leading to profound spiritual realization, independent of religious dogma or institutionalized belief systems.

In line with James's universalism, Walter Terence Stace (1886–1967), in *Mysticism and Philosophy*, divides mystical experiences into two broad categories: extrovertive (outward-turning) and introvertive (inward-turning).[6] These categories reflect the different ways one may experience the dissolution of the self and a sense of unity with the divine or the absolute.

In extrovertive mystical experiences, the person perceives unity in the external world. This means that the individual remains aware of the sensory world but perceives it in a radically transformed way. The ordinary distinctions between objects fade, and everything appears as interconnected or as manifestations of the One.

A common description of extrovertive mysticism might be the experience of seeing all of nature – trees, mountains, rivers, birds – as connected and unified with the divine essence, without losing the perception of individual objects.

In introvertive mystical experiences, on the other hand, someone turns profoundly inward and, perhaps by entering a deep meditative state, moves beyond sensory experience into a state of pure consciousness. In this state, the distinctions between self and world, subject and object, dissolve entirely, leading to a feeling of overwhelming unity or oneness with the absolute. It is often characterized by a profound stillness and silence.

Stace is well known for arguing that mystical experiences are universal across different religious and cultural traditions. He believed that while mystical experiences are interpreted through various cultural and religious lenses, the core experience – whether extrovertive or introvertive – is fundamentally the same and transcends specific religious doctrines. His universalism has been influential in the study of mysticism but has also been debated by scholars who more firmly emphasize the cultural and contextual aspects of mystical experiences.

Ralph W. Hood Jr. (1942–), the prominent psychologist of religion, developed his "Mysticism Scale," one of the most frequently used tools to measure mystical experiences across different religious traditions, based on the theoretical work of Stace. The scale also draws on the "four marks of mysticism" identified by James.

The Mysticism scale assesses various features of mystical experiences. It consists of a number of key parameters including ineffability, noetic quality, unity, transiency, inner subjectivity, and passivity, and consists of 32 statements. Respondents rate statements such as "I have had an experience in which I realized the oneness of all things"; "I have had an experience in which all things seemed to be part of a single whole"; and "I have had an experience that left me with a feeling of awe and reverence" on a Likert scale ranging from "strongly agree" to "strongly disagree."

Based on his research, Hood concludes: "Basically, mystical experiences in their most intense and generic form consist of an experience of ego loss in which the ego is in some sense merged with something greater than itself, yet somewhat similar to it also."[7]

Let us now turn to Jung's and Inayat Khan's self-reported experiences of the numinous.

In the case of Jung, we witness how his experiences led to a profound deepening of his understanding of the psyche. While his early career was rooted in scientific inquiry – marked by rigorous research, patient analysis, and merciless self-examination – he remained open to the irrational aspects of reality.

Through his studies of alchemy, he came to see the unconscious as a *process* of continuous transformation. It is the ego's relationship to the unconscious that drives psychological development.

Yet, his later experiences of awe and wonder led him to recognize the Self as the true center of the psyche – transcending the ego and reflecting a numinous, ineffable reality that some might equate with the divine.

Here is one abbreviated example from a full chapter in his autobiography, *Memories, Dreams, Reflections*, titled "Visions."

At the beginning of 1944 I broke my foot, and this misadventure was followed by a heart attack. In a state of unconsciousness I experienced deliriums and visions . . . The images were so tremendous . . . It seemed to me that I was high up in space. . . . The sight of the earth from this height was the most glorious thing I had ever seen. . . . A short distance away I saw in space a tremendous dark block of stone, like a meteorite. . . . An entrance led into a small antechamber. . . . As I approached . . . the entrance into the rock, a strange thing happened: I had the feeling that everything was being sloughed away; everything I aimed at or wished for or thought, the whole phantasmagoria of earthly existence, fell away or was stripped from me an extremely painful process. Nevertheless something remained; it was as if I now carried along with me everything I had ever experienced or done, everything that had happened around me. I might also say: history, and I felt with great certainty: this is what I am. "I am this bundle of what has been, and what has been accomplished. . . .

[When back to waking consciousness]. . . I asked the nurse to forgive me if she were harmed. There was such sanctity in the room, I said, that it might be harmful to her. Of course she did not understand me. For me the presence of sanctity had a magical atmosphere; I feared it might be unendurable to others. . . . This was it. There was a pneuma of inexpressible sanctity in the room, whose manifestation was the mysterium coniunctionis. I would never have imagined that any such experience was possible. . . . The visions and experiences were utterly real; there was nothing subjective about them; they all had a quality of absolute objectivity."

Jung, thus 69 years old, called back from the brink of death by his doctor, arrived at the conclusion that his illness, or rather the visions and experiences it engendered, had taught him that only through that objective cognition, detached from valuations, is the real *coniunctio* possible. He was free from his valuations of himself and of everything, ready to positively affirm whatever came on his path.

Jung's encounter with the numinous naturally impacted his further work and writings. Many of his principal works were written only henceforth, including his final book *Mysterium Coniunctionis: An Inquiry into the Separation and Synthesis of Psychic Opposites in Alchemy* (1957),[8] which he completed at the age of 80.

Let us now turn to Inayat Khan's journey and biographical rendering of his own mystical life. In his autobiography, Inayat Khan explains how he, as a young child, immersed himself in poetry and music; rhyme and rhythm.[9] His absorption was so strongly developed that when he started going to school he could not take any interest whatsoever in what was taught in class. Teachers were concerned, as were his parents, who believed there might be something wrong with the boy and feared that nothing would come of him. Only Inayat Khan's maternal grandfather Maula Bakhsh supported his real interests, individuality, and musical character. Then, when Inayat Khan was 14 years old, his grandfather passed away, and he was lost in grief and bereavement. Around the same time, his father received an assignment in Nepal, and he could come along. A one-year period of freedom – no school – and liberty to follow his own way began:

Sometimes I went on foot and sat on the rocks and thought about the deep things, wherever my mind would take me, wherever my feelings might take me. Whenever they were not stopped, I gave free expression to my thoughts and feelings. The openness of Nature made a free way for me to everything; so much freedom in my soul that it could reach up to the sun, the mountains, the hills and the trees, where there is no one to talk to, no one to trouble you, as one sits quietly listening to the sounds as they fall on the ear; the sounds of the wind, the waterfalls – so that one becomes one with Nature. It was like this all the time. My father did not know what I was really doing. He only knew that I was very fond of going about. But I did not know what I was doing either! Only this, that there was something in me which was being revealed, something that was becoming free, going out of me and meeting with something which belonged to it. Sometimes I recited verses. Sometimes I wrote songs, sometimes I hummed to myself. Sometimes I was quiet, sometimes I shed tears, sometimes I smiled for no apparent reason, as if nature was saying something to me with so much sympathy. It is as if we were not two, but one. Sometimes I was look-ing at it, and then closed my eyes, and there came such a peace, such calmness, such stillness – a vision of wonder – I knew not what it was that came about, except that the sorrow and sadness and loneliness produced by the passing of my grandfather was forgotten. Then after a year I returned home. . . . Even if I had no religion or vision or knew the meaning of things before, not knowing God, I still knew there was God, though I did not know who He was. Even if

I did not regard any object as sacred or worthy of reverence or worship, yet in my soul there was a tendency to revere something, to worship something.[10]

For Inayat Khan, this and countless further mystical experiences formed the foundation of his teachings, many of which are published in his collected works, *The Sufi Message*. In the volume *The Mysticism of Sound and Music* he emphasizes, "To me, architecture is music, gardening is music, farming is music, painting is music, poetry is music. In all the occupations of life where beauty has inspired, where the divine wine has been outpoured, there is music . . . because it is the exact miniature of the law, working with the whole universe."[11]

Hence, in his experience, realization of God and self-realization are natural consequences of deep devotion and openness to the divine. God revealed Himself to him through nature, music, art, and the senses. He reiterated how his experiences defied rational explanation yet resonated emphatically within his heart and soul and gradually built up a deep comprehension all the same.

As is evident from these examples, Jung and Inayat Khan entered into contact with the numinous from two different points in their lives, and their journeys could be described as reversed processes.

Jung, fully accomplished in his field of psychoanalysis, psychiatry, and with multiple publications on related themes, woke up to direct insight, awareness, and "knowing" of the Divine. Inayat Khan, on the other hand, was a young child when this knowing surfaced, and he had no studied reference point to frame it in. Nevertheless, the "knowing" persisted as his own to have and to seek amplification of through teachers, trainings, and educations.

Nevertheless, despite their differences in advances, from a hermeneutical perspective we can deduce that they both had noetic experiences and share in its transformative character, which they describe as ineffable, transitory, and as coming to them as a surprise and with a great mystery, a direct encounter with the numinous that impacted their respective outlook on life.

How to Understand Ephemeral Subjective Experiences of the Eternal Through Phenomenology of Consciousness

Most concisely, phenomenology of consciousness is a research method grounded in the exploration of lived experiences. It seeks to uncover how human beings, in their subjectivity, perceive and interpret the world, focusing on the structures of consciousness that shape our reality. When it comes to mystical or numinous experiences, such as those described by Jung and Inayat Khan, phenomenology helps us to understand how these deeply subjective experiences of the eternal manifest in consciousness.

In this section, we will explore experiences reported by Carl Jung and Hazrat Inayat Khan through the lens of key phenomenological thinkers and exemplify their relevance for understanding how Jung's and Inayat Khan's encounters with the numinous illuminate the deeper structures of their consciousness and yield insights that are instrumental in self-realization and individuation.

Jung's and Inayat Khan's Mystical Experiences: A Phenomenological Approach

Jung's near-death experience, as recounted in *Memories, Dreams, Reflections*, and Inayat Khan's mystical encounter with nature during his youth, both represent profound shifts in consciousness. These moments of contact with the numinous impacted their understanding of themselves and the world.

Jung's vision of a cosmic reality or Inayat Khan's immersion in nature shifted their respective moods and cognitions. While in the experience, they both desired to remain there, to intentionally move further into transcendent reality. Phenomenology provides a way to examine these experiences not just as isolated events but as part of the ongoing process of consciousness progressing toward greater awareness.

Edmund Husserl[12] (1859–1938), often considered the father of phenomenology, showed how consciousness is always about something; it is directed toward an object or experience. Consciousness possesses *intentionality*. In Jung's case, his consciousness during the vision was directed toward both a cosmic reality (the vision of Earth from space) and his personal reflection on his own life. Bracketing (epoché), Husserl's term for setting aside preconceived ideas of a phenomenon, helps us understand how Jung might have momentarily set aside his rational, scientific understanding of the world to fully experience the "objectivity," pure essence, of his vision. Similarly, Inayat Khan's youthful experience in nature allowed him to bracket his father's and societal expectations on intellectual understanding, leading to his direct encounter with the sacred.

Another common denominator reported by Jung and Inayat Khan is the here-ness, that is, their experiences were not abstract or detached; they were grounded in their specific contexts and lives. Jung's vision of being stripped of his earthly existence reveals the temporality and fragility of human life, while Inayat Khan's experience of unity with nature underscores a profound connection with the world around him. Martin Heidegger[13] (1889–1976) developed the concept of Being-in-the-world, which deepens our understanding of these mystical experiences. Heidegger emphasized the *temporal structure* of consciousness, meaning that consciousness is always immersed in time and that human beings are always situated in a world, and their consciousness is shaped by this context. Inayat Khan, already as a child, experienced time differently in his encounter with the numinous in nature, where the boundaries of past, present, and future dissolved into all-pervading being, existence, and his own aspect of that eternal being.

This leads us toward the embodiment of consciousness. Inayat Khan's emphasis on hearing, music, nature, and his sensory experience of *hearing the sounds of nature* as gateways to experiencing the divine aligns directly with Merleau-Ponty (1908–1961) saying that perception is not passive but that sensory experiences actively shape how we understand and interpret reality through embodied perception.[14] Inayat Khan's mystical experiences were mediated through his body's sensory engagement with the world.

Analogously, think of Jung's description of the awe and sacredness in the room, "an inexpressible pneuma" and "the odor of sanctity" – all very intense sensory experience, readily available, even when no longer tangible, yet having left an enduring feeling of awe and wonder. We find Jung's *Psychology and Alchemy*,[15] published 1944, the same year as his out-of-body experience, to involve sensory symbols such as colors, textures, and tastes described as metaphors for psychological transformation. Jung shows how the sensory phenomena described in alchemical texts, such as the color changes in the stages of the alchemical process, reflect how embodied experiences play a role in the process of individuation. Active imagination, a key Jungian technique, can be seen as a phenomenological method where sensory images serve as bridges between the conscious and unconscious realms.

Both Jung's and Inayat Khan's mystical experiences require interpretation to be integrated into their respective worldviews. Hans-Georg Gadamer (1900–2022) emphasized the importance of interpretation in human experience.[16] Gadamer's idea of horizons of understanding – helps to frame these numinous experiences as moments where the horizons of their past understanding were radically expanded. In Jung's case, his prior belief in the unconscious and his understanding of psychological archetypes shifted after his encounter with the divine. This can be understood as a fusion of horizons – the horizon of his prior analytical framework was fused with the horizon of the divine experience, transforming his understanding of the psyche. Inayat Khan's encounter with nature and the divine as a child expanded his understanding of God's presence in all things, and this deepened over time as he continued to experience and reflect on the signs of the divine, which he interpreted as examples of unity in existence. The interpretation of their respective experiences' intersubjectivity is served by the work of Dan Zahavi[17] (1967–) in which he stresses how relational consciousness informs self-awareness. In Inayat Khan's example of *Unity*, we see how his identity starts to form not as separate but as part of the relational whole of existence, where his self-awareness and awareness of the divine merge.

Both men engaged in dialogue – with themselves, their unconscious, the world around them, for instance in the form of art, and affectivity, the experience of inner life as a feeling – to make sense of what they each had encountered. This continuous reinterpretation allowed their experiences to shape not only their personal spiritual lives but also the teachings they offered to others.

By applying these five phenomenologists to examples of Carl Gustav Jung and Hazrat Inayat Khan, we can see how each thinker's method illuminates different aspects of mystical experience – whether it be intentionality, being, embodiment, relationality, or affectivity.

Notes

1 In South Asian usage, 'Khan' is traditionally a suffix indicating noble or warrior lineage, not used as a stand-alone personal name in formal reference.

2 Rudolf Otto, *The Idea of the Holy*, trans. John W. Harvey (Oxford: Oxford University Press, 1958), 13–14.
3 William James, *The Varieties of Religious Experience* (New York: Modern Library, 2002).
4 Leo Tolstoy, *My Confession* (Geneva, 1884. Publisher unknown).
5 Leo Tolstoy, *The Kingdom of God Is Within You*, trans. Constance Garnett (New York: Cassell Publishing Co., 1894).
6 Walter T. Stace, *Mysticism and Philosophy* (London: Macmillan, 1960), 131.
7 Ralph W. Hood, "Conceptual Criticisms of Regressive Explanations of Mysticism." *Review of Religious Research* 17, no. 3 (1976): 179–188.
8 C.G. Jung, *Mysterium Coniunctionis: An Inquiry into the Separation and Synthesis of Psychic Opposites in Alchemy*, 1st ed. (1955–1956).
9 Inayat Khan, *The Story of My Mystical Life*, reported by Dr. O.C. Gruner (Leeds, 10th June 1919), 5.
10 Inayat Khan, *The Story of My Mystical Life*, reported by Dr. O.C. Gruner (Leeds, 1919).
11 Hazrat Inayat Khan, *The Mysticism of Sound and Music, vol. 2 of The Sufi Message* (Delhi: Motilal Banarsidass, 1988), 74.
12 Edmund Husserl, *Ideas Pertaining to a Pure Phenomenology and to a Phenomenological Philosophy – Second Book: Studies in the Phenomenology of Constitution*, trans. R. Rojcewicz and A. Schuwer (Dordrecht: Kluwer, 1989).
13 Martin Heidegger, *Being and Time*, trans. John Macquarrie and Edward Robinson (New York: Harper & Row, 1962).
14 Maurice Merleau-Ponty, *Phenomenology of Perception*, trans. Donald A. Landes (London: Routledge, 2012), 243.
15 C.G. Jung, *Psychology and Alchemy*, trans. R. F. C. Hull, Bollingen Series XX (New York: Pantheon Books, 1953).
16 Hans-Georg Gadamer, *Truth and Method*, 2nd ed., trans. Joel Weinsheimer and Donald G. Marshall (New York: Continuum, 1989), 271.
17 Dan Zahavi, *Self-Awareness and Alterity: A Phenomenological Investigation* (Northwestern University Press, 1999).

Chapter 3

Carl Gustav Jung

Biography and Main Life Events

For Jung, the years spent pursuing the inner images that emerged from his unconscious were, as he later described, the most important period of his life – a formative experience that shaped everything that followed. The intensity of that time, with its overwhelming visions and inner struggles, became the foundation upon which his later scientific work and personal development would rest. It was a numinous beginning, a source from which both his professional theories and his life's trajectory would continually draw.

Carl Gustav Jung was born on July 26, 1875, in Kesswil, Switzerland, to Paul Achilles Jung and Emilie Preiswerk. Emilie was the youngest child of Samuel Preiswerk, who was head of the Reformed Clergy in Basel. Preiswerk was a religious scholar who specialized in Jewish, Hebrew, and Hebraic studies. Carl Gustav Jung's father, Paul, the son of a successful physician and dean of the University of Basel's Faculty of Medicine, was a student of Samuel Preiswerk when Paul studied Hebrew at Basel University.

Paul Jung joined the clergy himself and later became the local country parson for the Swiss Reformed Church in the small village of Kesswil, and as such, the family lived a meager existence. Soon after Carl's birth, his father was reassigned to a more prosperous parish in the village of Laufen, near the French border. Jung's upbringing in a religious Christian household, and his early connection to the natural world while growing up in rural environments, would later help to shape his philosophical views.

Carl's mother, Emilie, suffered from mental health issues, including depression. She nonetheless took an active interest in the occult and participated in spiritualist séances. She had frequent, intense spiritual and paranormal experiences and claimed that she was visited by spirits in her bedroom during the night. Jung himself recounts that one night, he observed a faintly luminous figure coming out of her room with a detached head floating in front of the figure.[1]

Emilie's mental instability contributed to tension between Jung's parents. At one point, Emilie was taken out of the home for several months for medical treatment at a nearby hospital. During this period, Carl lived with his aunt in Basel. The circumstances within the Jung household caused Carl to develop a closer relationship with his father than with his mother.

DOI: 10.4324/9781003431336-3

Figure 3.1 Carl Gustav Jung Portrait 1875–1961.
Source: © ETH Library Zurich, Image Archive/Portr_14163

It is, however, interesting to note that much later, in 1902, Carl Jung wrote his Ph.D. thesis in psychiatry *On the Psychology and Pathology of So-Called Occult Phenomena*. His supervisor was Eugene Bleuler, the director of the psychiatric hospital where Jung worked an internship, Burghölzli. This early research centered on a young woman exhibiting dissociative and paranormal behaviors, including mediumship. It laid the groundwork for Jung's exploration of the psyche, as it introduced him to the layers of the unconscious and symbolic manifestations in altered states.

Turning 12

At the age of 12, Jung got into an altercation at school with another boy and was violently pushed to the ground. The fall caused him to hit his head against the curbstone, and he reports that at the moment of impact, he thought in a flash "Now you don't have to go to school anymore." For some time afterward, he would occasionally faint while doing schoolwork or when walking to and from school. The doctors thought he might have epilepsy, and he was removed from school for six months of observation.

One day, Carl overheard his father speaking to a visitor about his condition and his future prospects. His father was genuinely concerned about his son's ability to support himself. This experience served as a wake-up call for Carl Gustav, who immediately dedicated himself to his schoolwork, realizing that achieving academic excellence was essential to his future. After this incident, Carl only fainted three more times. He later characterized his "fainting spells" as a neurosis, as opposed to a physiologically based condition linked to the original blow to the head on the schoolyard.[2]

Jung later described himself as an introverted child, often preferring solitude over interaction with his peers. He also became aware of two distinct personalities within him. Personality number one was his Swiss schoolboy persona. His second personality was that of an 18th-century man, who was dignified, authoritative, and influential.[3]

The foundation for Jung's principle of archetypes may have begun at a young age when he took a wooden ruler and carved one end of it into a tiny figure. He also painted a stone, placed both items into a pencil case, and hid them in the attic. He would occasionally write cryptic messages in a secret language on tiny pieces of paper and place them inside the same pencil case. Later on, as an adult, he stated that this ceremonial process made him feel safe and at peace. He drew a comparison between his intuitive and unconscious actions and the rituals of ancient cultures related to totems, all components of humanity's universal archetypes and collective unconscious.

Vocation and Family Life

With several family members being clergymen, Jung initially may have wanted to become a preacher or minister, but his ambition came to a firm end with his Holy Communion, which he experienced as very disappointing: nothing happened except a most hollow feeling came over him. "Why, that is not religion at all,"

I thought. "It is an absence of God; the church is a place I should not go to. It is not life which is there, but death," he recalls, while at the same time resisting the idea of having a relationship with God, let alone considering himself, his ego, as in any way analogous with God.[4]

Jung was an avid student of philosophy as a teenager, reading the likes of Kant, Schopenhauer, and Nietzsche. These philosophers helped form the basis of Jung's thinking and fundamentally influenced him throughout his life.

He was also interested in archaeology, but he could not pursue archaeology because the local University of Basel did not offer it. Instead, in 1895, he started studying medicine, and although his father passed away shortly thereafter, jeopardizing his funding, he graduated in 1900 at Basel University.

Jung married Emma Rauschenbach (1882–1955) in 1903 when he was 28 years old. Emma was the elder daughter of a wealthy industrialist, Johannes Rauschenbach-Schenck. Two years later, Johannes died, and his two daughters inherited the family enterprises, which ensured Jung's young family's future financial security. Emma's education was limited, but as the years went by, she became deeply involved in her husband's work and became a renowned psychoanalyst in her own right. Carl and Emma raised five children together, one boy and four girls. Emma took care of the children and the household, while Carl, in 1908–1909, built their house in Küsnacht, at the lake, where he saw patients in his private practice on the ground floor.

The Freud – Jung Drama

Jung had become interested in psychiatry while in medical school after reading *Psychopathia Sexualis* by Richard von Krafft-Ebing. During his internship in Burghölzli Hospital, Bleuler asked him to write a review of Freud's *The Interpretation of Dreams*. Jung soon became a qualified proponent of Freud's new "psycho-analysis." Jung then sent Freud a copy of his *Studies in Word Association* in 1906. Later that year, Jung published *Diagnostic Association Studies* and sent a copy to Freud.

In Vienna, in 1907, Carl Jung met the 20-year older Sigmund Freud for the first time. They spent an entire 13 hours together in lively conversation. Six months later, Freud sent a collection of his latest published essays to Jung in Zurich. This marked the beginning of six years of continual collaboration. During the early years of their association, the two men influenced each other.

Jung became enthralled by Freud's work, and they quickly developed a mentor/ protégé relationship. As Freud's chosen heir apparent, Jung was at the center of a revolution taking place in the world of psychology. That revolution was based on Freud's radical concept of the unconscious. As Jung's father had died when he was only 20, when Jung had to assume the responsibility for the welfare of his mother and nine years younger sister, to Jung, Freud was not simply a mentor. Freud, it has been said, also filled the vacuum of a father figure for Jung.

Victorian Age European society was highly civilized and rational, with an emphasis on strict codes of morality. This environment included social protocols regarding proper sexual behavior. It resulted in an epidemic of sexual repression.

Sigmund Freud, who was the leading psychoanalyst of his era, spent day after day listening to his patients, in particular his female patients, relate to him their fantasies and dreams. Freud concluded that people's behaviors were driven by repressed urges that they were totally unaware of, especially urges originating from their repressed sexuality. All of this was warehoused in the mind's unconscious and was the driving force in human behavior and personality.

Jung quickly embraced Freud's progressive ideas. The two became partners in promoting psychoanalysis throughout the world. Little by little, Freud's theories became accepted by mainstream medicine.

Freud believed that personality developed through a series of five childhood stages. If these five psychosexual stages were completed successfully, it resulted in a healthy personality. Psychosexual energy, or the "libido," he thought, was the driving force behind behavior. Early childhood development was understood to play a large role in personality development and, in his view, continued to influence a person's behavior as the individual grew into adulthood and matured. Freud had identified perhaps the biggest factor in personality development, that of human sexuality. After all, the urge to reproduce life is the most powerful force in the natural world, ensuring the continuation of all the various species of life.

In 1909, a landmark conference was convened at Clark University in Worcester, MA, to promote the burgeoning field of psychoanalysis. Freud and Jung, along with 27 distinguished psychiatrists, neurologists, and psychologists, were invited to attend at the conference. Freud presented Jung as his protégé, enabling Jung to meet with and forge alliances with the American colleagues.

A year later, Freud characterized Jung as "his adopted eldest son, his crown prince and successor,"[5] and in 1911 named him as president for life of the newly formed International Psychoanalytical Association. After some dissension from Freud's colleagues, Jung's tenure was reduced to two years. (8)

Under Freud's wing, Jung's future seemed secure. However, already in the course of their journey and the deeper Jung delved into Freud's theories, the more doubts and questions arose for him. He was puzzled by Freud's attitude to their shared dream analysis, and even more so by Freud's insistent and suggestive questions, which he did not experience as illuminating of anything else than that a rift between the two was afoot.

As Jung labored on his *Psychology of the Unconscious: A Study of the Transformations and Symbolisms of the Libido*, he felt the need to voice some of his disagreements with his mentor. At issue was the nature of the unconscious. Jung, impelled by a dream of a house, had come to believe, or know rather, that the unconscious contained not only personal repressed material (personal unconscious) but also a *collective unconscious* that held universal, archetypal symbols and patterns shared by all humanity, in particular the collective ideas and memories everyone inherits from their ancestors. This was the dream:

I found myself in a house I didn't recognize, though it was somehow 'mine'. I was in the upper floor – a salon filled with elegant, old-fashioned furniture in the rococo style. I thought, "Not bad," but realized I had never seen the lower levels. Curious, I went down to the ground floor. There, the atmosphere changed. The furnishings were older, from the fifteenth or sixteenth century. Room by room, I moved through the space, feeling drawn to explore further.

Eventually I came to a heavy door and opened it. Behind it was a stone stairway leading into a cellar. I descended again and entered a vaulted chamber that felt much older. The walls showed layers of brick and stone – I recognized them as Roman. Intrigued, I examined the floor, where I found a stone slab with a ring. Lifting it revealed another staircase. I followed it down into a narrow cave carved from rock.

Dust covered the ground, and scattered across it were bones and broken pottery, remnants of a primitive culture. I discovered two human skulls, obviously very old and half disintegrated.

Then I awoke.[6]

This dream became a pivotal moment in Jung's realization that the psyche was structured in layers, much like the house in his vision. The upper floors, adorned with familiar furnishings, represented the conscious mind – the personal identity shaped by culture and individual experience. But as he descended, he moved through progressively older strata, uncovering deeper, more ancient foundations of the psyche. The lowest chamber, filled with remnants of a primitive past, suggested a layer of mind untouched by personal history – something shared across generations. Jung later interpreted this as an analogy for the collective unconscious, a domain of inherited psychic structures and archaic images that shape human thought and behavior beyond individual memory. While Freud saw the unconscious primarily as a personal repository of repressed desires and conflicts, Jung came to view it as a vast and partly impersonal reservoir of symbols, myths, and ancestral knowledge.

The two men no doubt differed over *the nature* of the unconscious. Freud believed the unconscious was solely a storehouse of the individual's repressed emotions and desires, whereas Jung saw it on a much broader scale, transcending space and time. Over time, Jung refined this concept through extensive cross-cultural research, integrating material from alchemy, mythology, and world religions, all of which he saw as manifestations of these shared, universal patterns of the psyche.

Jung's realization that the unconscious extended beyond the personal led him to question other key aspects of Freud's psychoanalytic model, particularly the nature of libido. Freud had defined libido narrowly as a fundamentally sexual energy, the driving force behind human motivation and psychological conflict. But Jung, influenced by his studies of mythology, religion, and his own inner experiences, began to see this concept in a much broader light. If the unconscious was not simply a repository of repressed personal material but also a wellspring of universal symbols and archetypes, then libido, too, could not be reduced solely to sexuality. Instead, Jung conceived of it as a more general psychic energy – one that not only fueled instincts but also powered spiritual, creative, and symbolic dimensions of the psyche.

The rift between the two men came to a head in 1912 when Freud traveled from Vienna to visit a colleague in Kreuzlingen, without taking the trouble to travel the 50 miles by train to Zurich to visit Jung. Jung later referred to it as the "Kreuzlingen gesture." Jung then traveled to the U.S. to give a six-week series of lectures at Fordham University. The collected lectures were published in 1912 under the title *Psychology of the Unconscious*. The publication presented to its readers a clear delineation between Jung and Freud with regard to the libido, and Freud reacted vehemently to the publication of the Fordham University lectures. Jung would later state that the publication "cost me my friendship with Freud."[7]

Jung and Freud met personally one last time a year later at the Fourth International Psychoanalytical Congress in Munich. Afterward, Freud cut off all ties with Jung and they had no further association with one another. In one of his final letters to Freud, Jung's words reflect his level of exasperation:

> You go around sniffing out all the symptomatic actions in your vicinity, thus reducing everyone to the level of sons and daughters who blushingly admit the existence of their faults. Meanwhile you remain on top as the father, sitting pretty. For sheer obsequiousness nobody dares to pluck the prophet by the beard.[8]

On January 3, 1913, Freud replied "One who while behaving abnormally keeps shouting that he is normal gives ground for the suspicion that he lacks insight into his illness. I propose that we abandon our personal relations entirely. I shall lose nothing by it, for my only emotional tie with you has long been a thin thread – the lingering effect of past disappointments."[9]

In response, on January 6, Jung acknowledged Freud's wish, writing, "You yourself are the best judge of what this moment means to you. The rest is silence."[10]

The intensity of their break-up and its finality is palpable in these few lines alone.

Dropping Into and Confronting the Unconscious

Just a few short months after the break-up with Freud, World War I broke out and the entire collective European psyche became shattered. Jung retreated to his home in Küsnacht to fight his inner battles. He spent day after day sitting down at the shoreline of the lake in front of his house tossing pebbles into the water. He said he did not know why he was doing it except that it was the only thing he found that relieved his anxiety.

Jung fell into a period of years of disorientation and isolation in which he questioned his own sanity. He became deeply depressed, some say psychotic, experiencing incessant streams of fantasies, archetypal characters, and images from the unconscious. 1913–1916 was also a creative outpouring of dialogues with archetypal figures, which he recorded in journals: *The Black Books*.[11] *The Black Books* formed the basis for *The Red Book*, a major undertaking that he worked on until the 1930s.

Jung began to confront his own personal unconscious too and embarked on an extended period of deep self-analysis. He recorded his thoughts, analyzed his dreams, and made drawings, mandalas, that expressed the deep recesses of his unconscious. He also contemplated his future. He felt uncomfortable using Freud's terminology and methods if he was not going to practice Freud's system. He concluded that he had to create a system of his own. And it was through these deep and fundamentally life-changing experiences that Jung crafted what was to become the backbone of his later work, rooted in active imagination as the central process of the psyche. At the same time, in 1921, his earlier work on character structures, stimulated by his urge to explain why he and Freud had such differences in personality, resulted in his fundamental work: *Psychological Types*.[12]

During World War I, Jung was drafted as an army doctor, serving British officers and soldiers who had sought refuge in neutral Switzerland. He later traveled to England and began presenting his insights on analytical psychology and the collective unconscious.

Along with the end to World War I came a much more open society that was quick to embrace Jung's ideas, especially those involving individuality. For example, his *Psychological Types* quickly became an international best-seller. Everyone wanted to find out what their personality type was. At the age of 47, Jung suddenly found himself famous, and not just in Europe – he was recognized internationally. His practice in Küsnacht exploded with patients from all over the world writing and calling in for appointments a year in advance. Artists, poets, and writers all wanted to be associated with him and to be analyzed by him. At the same time, Jung embarked on extensive travels throughout Europe, the United States, Africa, and India. Jung's encounters with different cultures reinforced a conviction he had long held, but now experienced firsthand: human thought and behavior are shaped by forces that extend beyond the individual, rooted in the shared consciousness of entire civilizations – both past and present. Certain fundamental ideas, common to all peoples and cultures, have been passed down through generations, transcending race, religion, and geography. This collective unconscious, he said, compels humanity toward similar patterns of thought and action, even as they take on diverse expressions across different societies.

Engaging With the Deeply Dark Side of the Shadow

Much of his travels and work was put on hold as, throughout the 1930s, Europe began marching again toward another war. Jung became controversial when he held that, in addition to a shared human heritage, there were inherent psychological differences between cultural groups, such as Jews, Aryans, and Chinese. Although criticized, he held his ground, insisting that everyone could and should learn about others' differences to foster peace and understanding. Nonetheless, between 1933 and 1936 Jung participated in antisemitic gatherings in Germany and spoke out against Jews, stereotyping the Jewish psyche as "nomadic," and so aligning with ideas of national and racial identity popular in German-speaking intellectual circles. This period of time correlated with the rise of National Socialism, Adolf Hitler's far-right totalitarian socio-political ideology: Nazism.

For a nuanced understanding of Jung's stance on Jewish people and his public statements – potentially fueled by the collective shadow of his time – one must also consider his actions. For instance, while in Germany, he appointed Jewish analysts to prominent positions and continued professional relationships with Jewish students and analysts even when doing so could, at least, have risked his career. Jung furthermore hired a Jewish lawyer named Rosenbaum to introduce a large number of loopholes into the Nazis' antisemitic regulations.[13] After the end of World War II, he apologized for his words and wrote articles and letters opposing any association with the Nazis and denouncing the antisemitic and Nazi regime.

In an emotional letter to Mary Mellon, who was the founder of the Bollingen series, which published Jung's *Collected Works* in English, on September 24, 1945, Jung wrote:

> On account of my critique of the German tyranny, I was on the black list of Gestapo, and if the Germans had invaded Switzerland, I would certainly have been put on the spot. Well-informed Germans told me so. My pupils in Germany were forced to repudiate my views publicly. I tell you these things, because you probably have heard the absurd rumor that I am a Nazi. This rumor has been started by Freudian Jews in America. Their hatred of myself went as far as India, where I found falsified photo's [sic] in the Psychological Seminar of Calcutta University . . . I have challenged the Nazis already in 1934 at a great reception in Frankfort in the house of Baron Schnitzler, the Director of the I.G. Farben concern. I told them that their 'anticlockwise Swastika' is whirling down into the abyss of unconsciousness and evil. And this prediction has come off – 'and how!'[14]

After the war, Jung stopped treating individual patients and concentrated his time on traveling and lecturing. His supporters pleaded with him to found an institute to present his theories. Jung, who was not in favor, argued that individuation is a process of differentiation aimed at the development of the individual personality standing on his or her own feet, adding that "All collective identities, such as membership in organizations, support of 'isms' and so on, interfere with fulfillment of this task. Such collective identities are crutches for the lame, shields for the timid, beds for the lazy, nurseries for the irresponsible. . . ."[15] He was opposed to anyone following him or following anyone else for that matter.

Yet, he continued to hold the Eranos gatherings in high esteem, valuing them as a unique confluence of intellectual and spiritual exploration. These annual conferences, initiated in 1933 by Olga Fröbe-Kapteyn in Ascona, Switzerland, were envisioned as a platform where Eastern and Western philosophies could engage in meaningful dialogue. Among notable participants were Karl Kerényi, a classical philologist, and Henry Corbin, the well-known Islamic philosopher, and, as pictured here,[16] (From left) [unidentified person,] Gershom Scholem, Julie

Figure 3.2 (From left) [unidentified person,] Gershom Scholem, Julie Blumenfeld-Neumann, Erich Neumann, Carl Gustav Jung, Mircea Eliade, John David ("Jack") Barrett, Jr., and (probably) Vaun Gillmor at the Eranos Round Table, on the terrace of Casa Gabriella, in August 1950.

Blumenfeld-Neumann, Erich Neumann, Carl Gustav Jung, Mircea Eliade, John David ("Jack") Barrett, Jr., and (probably) Vaun Gillmor at the Eranos Round Table, on the terrace of Casa Gabriella, in August 1950. Aniela Jaffé, Jung's close collaborator and biographer, recounted in her writings the profound impact these gatherings had on Jung and vice versa.

Jung nevertheless always stressed the importance of the individual. Yet, he understood that people needed a formal setting in which to learn, feel at home, and be nourished in their growth, and, so, eventually he reluctantly agreed. Institutes bearing his name were opened in various cities around the world, including San Francisco, Buenos Aires, Kiev, and Singapore.

In 1943, Jung became a full professor of medical psychology at the University of Basel. But his heart attack a year later, and subsequent near-death experience, prompted him to resign to lead a more private and contemplative life with family and friends. He continued to publish books and papers all the way up to the date of his death, including a number of publications which came into print posthumously.

Jung died on June 6, 1961, at Küsnacht after a short circulatory-related illness. He was 85.

Notes

1 Carl G. Jung, *Memories, Dreams, Reflections*, ed. Aniela Jaffé, trans. Richard and Clara Winston (New York: Vintage, 1989), 18.

2 Jung, *Memories, Dreams, Reflections,* 33.

3 Jung, *Memories, Dreams, Reflections,* 33–34.

4 Jung, *Memories, Dreams, Reflections*, 55–57.

5 Sigmund Freud and Carl Jung, *The Freud/Jung Letters: The Correspondence between Sigmund Freud and C.G. Jung*, ed. William McGuire, trans. Ralph Manheim and R. F. C. Hull (Cambridge, MA: Harvard University Press, 1974), 218.

6 Jung, *Memories, Dreams, Reflections*, 158–160.

7 Jung, *Memories, Dreams, Reflections*, 167.

8 Carl G. Jung, Letter to Sigmund Freud, November 25, 1912, in *The Freud/Jung Letters: The Correspondence between Sigmund Freud and C.G. Jung*, ed. William McGuire, trans. Ralph Manheim and R. F. C. Hull (Princeton, NJ: Princeton University Press, 1974), 546–547.

9 Sigmund Freud, Letter to Carl G. Jung, January 3, 1913, in *The Freud/Jung Letters: The Correspondence between Sigmund Freud and C.G. Jung*, ed. William McGuire, trans. Ralph Manheim and R. F. C. Hull (Princeton, NJ: Princeton University Press, 1974), 540–541.

10 "The rest is silence" is a reference to *Hamlet*. These are Hamlet's final words before he dies in Act V. In the context of the play, it signifies Hamlet's resignation and acceptance of fate as he succumbs to the end of his journey. The phrase suggests an end to both his personal turmoil and the existential questions that haunt him, transitioning into the unknown.

11 C. G. Jung, *The Black Books 1913–1932: Notebooks of Transformation*, ed. Sonu Shamdasani, trans. Martin Liebscher, John Peck, and Sonu Shamdasani (New York: W. W. Norton & Company, 2020).

12 A typology that serves as the basis for the world's most used personality test; The Meyer-Briggs Type Index, commonly known as the MBTI.

13 Daniel Burston, *Anti-Semitism and Analytical Psychology: Jung, Politics and Culture* (New York: Routledge, 2021).

14 William Schoenl, *C.G. Jung: His Friendships with Mary Mellon and J.B. Priestley* (Wilmette, IL: Chiron Publications, 1998).

15 Jung, *Memories, Dreams, Reflections*, 342.

16 I am indebted to the Fondazione Eranos, Ascona, for granting the permission to publish the photograph taken by Ph. Margarethe Fellerer. Eranos Foundation Archives. All rights reserved.

Chapter 4

Individuation

A Lifelong Journey

"Individuation" is the complex theme chosen for this book to be held up against Inayat Khan's theme of "Self-realization." It is also central to Jung's analytical psychology as it weaves together fundamental concepts pertaining to Jung's entire oeuvre. It essentially signifies the process that every person undergoes throughout life in the quest for wholeness. It is important to bear in mind that individuation evolves in a circular manner. Hence, although certain steps may occur in a certain sequence, similar to us learning to walk before running and not the other way around, these steps nevertheless remain part and parcel of that lifelong individuation. A second fact to observe is that, not seldom, a hindrance to individuation, say, "vanity," once fully tackled and renounced, may pop up at the most undesirable moment and with the greatest, if not shocking, impact. It happens to the best, to all of us.

In the following, I acknowledge that aspects of individuation occur simultaneously rather than chronologically. The modalities of individuation that I have chosen to illustrate it with – active imagination, alchemy, synchronicity, and numinosity – are thus not meant to build up to a crescendo with the numinous as the apex of the individuation goal. In fact, I personally believe that individuation wouldn't really be ignited without a numinous experience, in whatever form, and that synchronicity occurs in its own good time as alchemical awareness comes and goes. What if life's journey is as much a dream, a fantasy, an imagination, as it is concrete reality?

The Red Book is my starting point – because, in Jung's own words, "Everything else is to be derived from this," and "My entire life consisted in elaborating what had burst forth from the unconscious . . ."[1]

I will also briefly reflect on how his central theories and concepts developed through collaboration with his wife and close colleagues, and how we now have access to them through fundamental works including *Psychological Types* (1921), *Two Essays on Analytical Psychology* (1928), *Symbols of Transformation* (1952, revised from *Psychology of the Unconscious*, 1912), *Psychology and Alchemy* (1944), *Aion: Researches into the Phenomenology of the Self* (1951), and *Mysterium Coniunctionis: An Inquiry into the Separation and Synthesis of Psychic Opposites in Alchemy* (1955).[2]

Let us start with active imagination, the chief process (method, technique) on the journey of individuation.

DOI: 10.4324/9781003431336-4

Figure 4.1 Jung, Carl Gustav, 26.7.1875 – 6.6.1961, Suisse medic/physician and psychologist, sitting at the desktop, working, beginning 1940s, C.G., founder of analytical psychology, Jungian psychology, smoking, pipe, reading, cap, headdress.

Source: INTERFOTO/Alamy Stock Photo.

Active Imagination

Jung's discovery of active imagination as a technique for individuation was primarily triggered by his own need for self-exploration following his split with Freud in 1913. As we have seen, the break landed him in intense inner turmoil and psychic disorientation, prompting him to seek ways to engage directly with his unconscious, and not in a tried and tested way, such as "free association" aimed at uncovering repressed content. Jung desperately needed to be carried forward, rather than confronting content repressed in the past.

The method is rooted in intentionally allowing images from the unconscious to surface uncensored, without any valuation, and to engage in dialogue with characters as they appear. This technique came to Jung also partly thanks to medieval alchemical texts, which he had begun studying around the same time. He was struck by how alchemists symbolized their own psychological processes through images and figures, an approach that resonated with what he was experiencing internally.

Alchemy, with its strange imagery of *nigredo*, *albedo*, and *rubedo*, was a symbolic record of transformation, revealing in veiled language the same process Jung was experiencing in his inner dialogues. Active imagination gave him the practice and set the process going, while alchemy provided the mirror, a symbolic vocabulary for individuation. Jung, referring to the alchemist Gerhard Dorn, established that the purpose of both individuation and the Opus was to unite with the One, and that one can never find that One except by first becoming one within oneself.

Thus, in Jung's life, active imagination and alchemy belonged together and converged: one as the experiential method, the other as the symbolic archive.

Hic Rhodus, Hic Salta!

Jung marks the moment of diving into his "most difficult experiment":

> It was during Advent of the year 1913 – December 12, to be exact – that I resolved upon the decisive step. I was sitting at my desk once more, thinking over my fears. Then I let myself drop. Suddenly it was as though the ground literally gave way beneath my feet, and I plunged into the dark depths.[3]

What happened next has been richly described and interpreted by scholars and Jungians alike. To Jung himself, it was a gruesome necessity only made possible by Emma, his wife, and his practice, whose stability ensured he would not forever swirl around in lonely psychosis, and in the inner cosmos he crafted through his consistent active imagination experiment.

> It is of course ironical that I, a psychiatrist, should at almost every step of my experiment have run into the same psychic material which is the stuff of psychosis and is found in the insane. This is the fund of unconscious images which fatally confuse the mental patient. But it is also the matrix of a mythopoeic

imagination which has vanished from our rational age. Though such imagination is present everywhere, it is both tabooed and dreaded, so that it even appears to be a risky experiment or a questionable adventure to entrust oneself to the uncertain path that leads into the depths of the unconscious . . . The unconscious contents could have driven me out of my wits. But my family, and the knowledge: I have a medical diploma from a Swiss university, I must help my patients, I have a wife and five children, I live at 228 Seestrasse in Küsnacht – these were actualities which made demands upon me and proved to me again and again that I really existed.[4]

In addition to overwhelming unconscious images, his own excessive thoughts and thinking brought him into a state of depletion. In this phase of his journey toward his soul, his experiences are as follows:

Through the turning of my desire from things and men, I turned my self away from things and men, but that is precisely how I became the secure prey of my thoughts, yes, I wholly became my thoughts.

I also had to detach myself from my thoughts through turning my desire away from them. And at once, I noticed that my self [sic] became a desert, where only the sun of unquiet desire burned. I was overwhelmed by the endless infertility of this desert.

. . .

After a hard struggle I have come a piece of the way nearer to you. How hard this struggle was! I had fallen into an undergrowth of doubt, confusion, and scorn. I recognize that I must be alone with my soul. . .

My soul answered and said, "You speak to me as if you were a child complaining to its mother. I am not your mother." I do not want to complain, but let me say to you that mine is a long and dusty road. You are to me like a shady tree in the wilderness. I would like to enjoy your shade. But my soul answered, "You are pleasure-seeking. Where is your patience? Your time has not yet run its course. Have you forgotten why you went into the desert?[5]

Jung continues his dialogue with his soul in the same vein: "I am poor and empty," "I would like to sit down near you and at least feel the breath of your animating presence," "All day long, sandy, dusty paths," "Once I despaired of myself, as you know."

Finally, after having (self-)concedingly laid down his vanity, night twenty-five brings solace to his torment: "This is how long it took my soul to awaken from a shadowy being to her own life, until she could approach me as a free-standing being separate from me. And I received hard but salutary words from her."[6]

Surely, Jung's barren-desert realization of his demanding persona and painful aspects of his shadow in the form of grandiosity, vanity, and self-pity combined took him a step further toward individuation.

Then, a most important moment in Jung's individuation process came to him through a dream,

> There was a blue sky, like the sea, covered not by clouds but by flat brown clods of earth. It looked as if the clods were breaking apart and the blue water of the sea were becoming visible between them. But the water was the blue sky. Suddenly there appeared from the right a winged being sailing across the sky. I saw that it was an old man with the horns of a bull. He held a bunch of four keys, one of which he clutched as if he were about to open a lock. He had the wings of the kingfisher with its characteristic colors.[7]

Jung did not understand this dream image. Yet it ushered him forward, and for some days he worked on painting the dream image to retain it in memory. In that time, to his stunned amazement, in his garden by the lake shore, he found a dead kingfisher! Kingfishers are rare in the vicinity of Zurich, and to find a dead one was a unique experience for Jung. This obvious sign of synchronicity – a meaningful coincidence[8] – initiated an active imagination dialogue that was to be formative for much of Jung's understanding of the unconscious. It revealed to him significant archetypal figures inhabiting his unconscious, and through his encounters and interactions with them, he gradually started to feel safe and nourished also in that realm.

It turned out that the old man with the horns of a bull was named Philemon, and that Philemon was an emanation of the prophet Elijah. Philemon, who was a pagan with an Egypto-Hellenistic atmosphere, became Jung's guide and bestowed upon him superior insight and wisdom. This did not occur in a tutorial manner, rather

> brought home to me the crucial insight that there are things in the psyche which I do not produce, but which produce themselves and have their own life. Philemon represented a force which was not myself. In my fantasies I held conversations with him, and he said things which I had not consciously thought. For I observed clearly that it was he who spoke, not I.[9]

Their dialogues often took place in Jung's garden and imparted awareness of objectivity, that is, that the unconscious bestows insights that consciousness is yet to apprehend, and that the psyche has objective reality. Philemon explained the latter with a metaphor, telling Jung that he treats his thoughts as if they were "his," as if he had generated them out of himself, whereas in Philemon's view, thoughts were like animals in the forest, or people in a room, or birds in the air, saying, "If you should see people in a room, you would not think that you had made those people, or that you were responsible for them."[10]

At the same time, Jung became aware of his own separate and distinct being in relation to Philemon. Jung's dance between "me" and "he" gradually narrowed down to a voice in which "me" is more distinct from "he." In the *First Sermon to the Dead*, the third part of *The Red Book*, Jung is again reminded of the necessity of becoming a distinct individual and aware of his unique existence, separate from everything else. This is when Philemon explains the nature of the pleroma, the vast sea of all that is – Creation – and reiterates that not differentiating means nothing less than death! "Creatures came into being, but not creation: since creation is the very quality of the Pleroma, as much as noncreation, eternal death. Creation is ever-present, and so is death. The Pleroma has everything, differentiation and nondifferentiation . . . Differentiation is creation. It is differentiated. Differentiation is its essence, and therefore it differentiates. Therefore man differentiates, since his essence is differentiation."[11]

So, although Jung demonstrates his being solidly differentiated, it is worth remembering that a collective arousal in Europe, and particularly German-speaking Europe, got the better of him for some time, and his grandiose and inferior shadow found a platform for expression, which he later was graceful enough to admit and regret fervently. "I am sorry" pinches not only the ego, but underneath the persona, also the shadow.

Jung thus far reveals how his discovery of active imagination initiated dramatic shifts in his awareness of the unconscious, his persona, the mask presented to the world, and his personal shadow meaning *both* his self-congratulating, pathetic side, as well as his energetic, forward-striving ingenuity.

Jung refers to the aftermath of the break with Freud as a state of disorientation, accompanied by multiple dreams, many of which made no sense to him. He recounts one that played a role in his healing as follows:

I dreamt at that time (it was shortly after Christmas 1912) that I was sitting with my children in a marvelous and richly furnished castle apartment – an open columned hall – we were sitting at a round table, whose top was a marvelous dark green stone. Suddenly a gull or a dove flew in and sprang lightly onto the table. I admonished the children to be quiet, so that they would not scare away the beautiful white bird. Suddenly this bird turned into a child of eight years, a small blonde girl, and ran around playing with my children in the marvelous columned colonnades. Then the child suddenly turned into the gull or dove. She said the following to me: 'Only in the first hour of the night can I become human, while the male dove is busy with the twelve dead'. With these words the bird flew away and I awoke.[12]

As Jung mulled over its meaning, he gradually came to realize that the past, his past, was not dead but wide awake and alive in his present here and now. His submission to the impulses in his unconscious, as a result of this particular dream, led him to the recollection of how he, as an 11-year-old boy, was immersed in playing with building blocks, making small houses and castles. He reluctantly realized that now he was called to pick up that play and again build such fantasy houses.

He had no other option but to return to that child's world and take up his small, seemingly trivial play once again. Though this marked a decisive turning point in my life, I yielded only after prolonged resistance and with deep reluctance. For Jung it was a bitter and humiliating realization that there was nothing left for him to do except play childish games.[13]

This example of Jung's "painfully humiliating experience" is not only an illustration of how the shadow feels but also of its resourcefulness – its creative contribution to conscious life.

Emma stood by Jung with a solid, unwavering commitment – from the day she married him at 21 until her death 52 years later, in 1955. Only three times did she threaten divorce! According to their children, Carl depended profoundly on her support – both for his life and for his work.[14] Posterity owes much to her.

Thanks to Emma's grounding presence, his clinical practice, and his ongoing engagement with active imagination, Jung gradually and laboriously detached himself from persona identifications. In the alchemical process of *separatio* – of differentiation – he sought to free himself even from the *pleroma*, the undivided beginning and end of creation.

As we will see, through this same alchemical process – partly stimulated by synchronistic events – Jung developed an ever-deepening affinity with the archetypes dwelling in the collective unconscious. These were not mere symbols but real presences with whom he established relationships. Philemon, his wise inner guide, grew into an objective reality, much like Virgil was to Dante or Athena to Odysseus, for whom too their inner guide was their own *metis*.

Active imagination, as a practice, has a dreamlike quality, though it unfolds in a state of consciousness. To conclude this exploration of active imagination, let us step even closer to Jung himself as a practitioner of the method he discovered. What might it be like when he engaged in this process?

Let's say one night, Jung has a dream in which he is walking through his home, the familiar place where he has lived with his family for so many years. Yet, in the dream, he feels inexplicably drawn to a staircase – one he rarely uses in daily life. It is meant for the housekeeper, who sometimes hangs the washing there in winter. But now, in this dream, he cannot resist climbing those old, narrow steps.

He grasps the wooden handrail on his left and ascends, each step requiring a little more effort. As he nears the top, he finds himself standing in the dimness of the upper landing. The space is unfamiliar, almost forgotten. He searches for a light switch but cannot recall where it is – or if one even exists.

Then, on his left, he notices it: a thin sliver of dimmed light seeping from beneath a door. He steps forward and pushes it open.

Inside, a single candle flickers on an ornate baroque table, casting long shadows across the room. As he moves closer, his gaze is drawn to a book – beautifully bound in emerald-green leather, with a golden lock clasped at its center. As he reaches for the book, a scent catches him off guard – something familiar yet unplaceable. The recognition tugs at him, distracting him just enough that he wakes up. Intrigued, energized, and filled with curiosity, he immediately writes down the dream in a black book, capturing every detail while it is still fresh.

During breakfast, he shares his dream with Emma, making it even more vivid in his waking mind. Then, he turns to the duties of the day – his practice, his patients, the steady rhythm of scheduled sessions.

After dinner, once the children are in bed and the house has fallen quiet, he retreats to his study. Sitting at his desk, looking out the window at the lake, he allows himself to enter the world of imagination. The book appears once more, and he feels compelled to open it. As he begins to read, each word shimmers softly, gently like tiny crystals. Then, in a flash, the entire open pages burst forth with radiant white light. In that very moment, he realizes that the words he read have entered his mind and heart and forever made an imprint on him. His experience of awe and wonder overtakes him as he senses something metamorphosing within. Then, the right page turned and with a whisper, like the breath of all that is, it pronounced his name.

Alchemy

For Jung, alchemy served as the symbolic language for the process of individuation and a bridge between the conscious and the unconscious. He saw the alchemists' work – the transformation of base metals into gold – as an analogy for the transformation of consciousness. In alchemical texts, he identified symbols and imagery that he believed mirrored stages of inner development, such as the *coniunctio*, or the *chymical wedding*, where opposites unite.

A key part of this process involves integrating the contrasexual aspects of the psyche – the *anima*, or inner feminine in a man, and the *animus*, or inner masculine in a woman. These archetypal figures represent the unconscious, binary aspect of the psyche, and they frequently appeared in alchemical symbols, such as the union of Sol and Luna (sun and moon), which Jung interpreted as symbolic of reconciling inner dualities.

Jung's interest in alchemy was sparked by his study of ancient texts that seemed to portray unconscious processes similar to those he observed in his own experiment and reported in *The Red Book*. His studies in alchemy and his personal experiences reflecting alchemical processes culminated in the works *Psychology and Alchemy* and *Mysterium Coniunctionis*, a study of the alchemical process as a metaphor for the union of opposites within the psyche and individuation.

The *anima* and the *animus*, respectively, the syzygy, are in terms of the structure of the psyche located further below the persona and the shadow, that is, more unconscious. In an effort, nevertheless, to see those figures surface, we tend to, unconsciously mostly, project their character upon a romantic partner, so that the partner may manifest the *anima* or *animus,* making them available for integration. As satisfying as this sounds and might be, anyone who has been romantically involved in a major relationship knows such integration can be complex. It was no different for Jung. Let us get right into it through *The Red Book* chapter titled *Mysterium. Encounter* which opens as follows,

On the night when I considered the essence of God, I became aware of an image: I lay in a dark depth. An old man stood before me. He looked like one of the old prophets. A black serpent lay at his feet. Some distance away, I saw a house with columns. A beautiful maiden stepped out of the door. She walked uncertainly, and I saw that she was blind. The old man waved to me, and I followed him to the house at the foot of the sheer wall of rock. The serpent crept behind us.

Darkness reigned inside the house. We entered a high hall with glittering walls. Suddenly a door opened onto a garden full of bright sunshine. We stepped outside, and the old man said, "Do you know where you are?"

"I am a stranger here and everything seems strange to me, anxious as in a dream. Who are you?"

"I am Elijah, and this is my daughter Salome."

"The daughter of Herod, the bloodthirsty woman?"

"Why do you judge so? You see she is blind. She is my daughter . . . My wisdom and my daughter are one."

I was shocked, unable to grasp it.

Elijah continued: "Consider this: Her blindness and my sight have made us companions through eternity."

"Forgive my astonishment, am I truly in the underworld?"

Salome then spoke: "Do you love me?"

I recoiled, overwhelmed: "How can I love you? I see only one thing – you are Salome, a tiger, stained with the blood of the holy one."

"You will love me," she answered.

I continued resisting her, caught in a spiral of fear and confusion, questioning why I was here at all.

Elijah's voice rose once more: "By her love, shall you know her."

I was horrified."[15]

The shadow is, as we have seen, difficult to face, digest, and integrate because it brings up resistance. The subjectively favored self-image, the persona, has a hard time assimilating the shadow and making it part of an expanded self-image.

In the case of Jung, the *anima*, however, posed a bigger challenge because she did not bring up only resistance but repulsion, disgust, and *thanatophobia* – death anxiety.

But the alchemical mystery now started had its own course. Jung fled into his psychological stronghold: thinking. Elijah seemed to be the most reasonable of the three and to have a clear intelligence, so Jung held on to him. The snake, he says, "displayed unmistakable fondness" of him.[16]

I see how the black serpent writhes up the tree, and hides in the branches. Everything becomes gloomy and doubtful. Elijah rises, I follow and we go silently back through the hall. Doubt tears me apart. It is all so unreal and yet a part of my longing remains behind. Will I come again? Salome loves me, do I love her? I hear wild music, a tambourine, a sultry moonlit night, the bloody-staring head of the holy one – fear seizes me. I rush out. I am surrounded by the dark night. It is pitch black all around me.[17]

While reflecting on his conundrum – thinking, logos, versus feeling, eros, and how these two aspects within himself produce such intense conflict, he concludes that forethinking, determined thoughts, only bring the chaotic into form and definition; it does not alleviate the tension. Pleasure, on the other hand, loves the form it assumes. Elijah represents the forethinker, Salome pleasure. Here is an example of Jung's exercise in forethinking,

> The forethinker is a seer, but pleasure is blind. It does not foresee, but desires what it touches. Forethinking is not powerful in itself and therefore does not move. But pleasure is power, and therefore it moves. Forethinking needs pleasure to be able to come to form. Pleasure needs forethinking to come to form, which it requires.[18]

Eventually, Jung found the serpent to be a third principle, associated with both Elijah and Salome yet not part of them. Hence, the black serpent showed Jung the unconditional difference in essence between the two principles in him which must be united, as a station in the individuation process.

Much later in *The Red Book*, in *Scrutinies*, he meets the black serpent again – this time entwined with a red serpent.[19] "I see how the black serpent lies before me. Then the red serpent comes up, it rises, and then they struggle. The red serpent overcomes the black, it binds itself around my body, and I am covered in its reddish glow." For Jung, this vision dramatized the transition from *nigredo* (blackness, heaviness, despair) to *rubedo* (the reddening, the fullness of transformation, manifesting the Self). It discloses the ongoing, never-final process of individuation: the painful struggle of coming to terms with inner opposites – not once and for all, but as a continuous work of transformation as the psyche moves toward wholeness. As Elijah, Salome, and "I" (Jung) endure their continued unrelenting dialogue, it culminates in Jung's felt sense of crucifixion. This experience is then followed by redemption and transformation of all three parties. Salome regains sight, Elijah turns into a huge flame of white light, and Jung is united, or at least provisionally reconciled, with his anima, his inner feminine half – his feelings.

> It is as if I stood alone on a high mountain with stiff outstretched arms. The serpent squeezes my body in its terrible coils and the blood streams from my body, spilling down the mountainside. Salome bends down to my feet and wraps her black hair round them. She lies thus for a long time. Then she cries, "I see light!" Truly, she sees, her eyes are open. The serpent falls from my body and lies languidly on the ground. I stride over it and kneel at the feet of the prophet, whose form shines like a flame.
>
> E: Your work is fulfilled here.[20]

Jung's anima integration process was, however, to continue "on the other side," (t)here, in conscious life with a woman of flesh and blood. In 1913, Jung embarked on a relationship with Toni Wolff.

Antonia Wolff (1888–1953) had been a patient of his, brought to him by her mother in 1910. Toni suffered from a heavy depression caused by her father's death, and Jung treated her for this for a little over a year. The therapy, largely delving into their common ground in mythology, astrology, and symbolism, was successful, and Toni was cured enough to join Jung at the Weimar Congress and moved on to conduct research and assist Jung in his.

According to Sonu Shamdasani, Jung noted in *Black Book 2*, that it was the earlier mentioned dream with the gull or a dove that turned into a small girl of 8 years old that made him decide to enter what would become a 30-year-long relationship with Toni Wolff as his companion in the unconscious realm and as his second wife.[21]

Toni Wolff, who later became an esteemed psychoanalyst, was instrumental in Jung's development of key concepts related to the individuation process – persona, shadow, animus, and anima. She also contributed to Jung's theory of psychological types, published in *Psychological Types*.[22] Her studies related to those notions resulted in numerous papers and one book, *Structural Forms of the Feminine Psyche*, in which she defines four typologies of the feminine psyche: the Amazon, the Mother, the Hetaira, and Medial Woman. Toni herself likely identified with the Hetaira type, the woman who is a companion and

> is instinctively related to the personal psychology of the male. . . . The function of the Hetaira is to awaken the individual psychic life in the male and to lead him through and beyond his male responsibilities towards the formation of a total personality. The Hetaira thus affects the shadow side of the male and the subjective side of the anima – a problem which is not without danger.[23]

Jung's ambition, however, remained to establish an independent relationship with his anima, to free himself from her spell. And, perhaps of his own accord, it was accomplished.

Jung speaks about how for decades he had always turned to the anima when he felt that his emotional behavior was disturbed, and that something had been constellated in the unconscious. He would then ask the anima: "Now what are you up to? What do you see? I should like to know." After some resistance, she regularly produced an image. As soon as the image was there, his unrest or sense of oppression vanished, and the whole energy of these emotions was transformed into interest in and curiosity about the image. He would speak with the anima about the images she communicated to him, for he had to try to understand them just like a dream. Later in life, Jung no longer found it necessary to engage the anima in dialogue, as the emotional disturbances that once made such exchanges essential had fallen away. Still, had those emotions returned, he would have approached them in the same way. By then, he had learned to accept the contents of the unconscious and to understand them. He had become directly conscious of the anima's ideas and knew how to relate to the inner images.[24]

The significance of alchemy for the individuation process can hardly be overrated. In fact, Jung says that he discovered the correspondence between his strictly subjective experiences of the collective unconscious and its archetypes, as detailed in *The Red Book*, and the principles and processes outlined in alchemy, which he had deep understanding of through studies of 16th-century alchemists Paracelsus's and Gerhard Dorn's work. In *Psychology and Alchemy,* he demonstrates this correspondence: "I can read their meaning directly from my dreams, and therefore no longer need a mediator to communicate them," he said.[25]

A large part of Jung's work revolves around the study of the problem of opposites and especially their alchemical symbolism. As we have seen, the pair of anima and animus form a critical component of the individuation process. In Jung's case, his inner feminine base forms a bridge between his subjective consciousness on the one hand and the collective unconscious on the other. At the same time, the anima is a Soul figure and, as such, only part of consciousness even when recognized as Soul.

> I was greatly intrigued by the fact that a woman should interfere with me from within. My conclusion was that she must be the "soul," in the primitive sense, and I began to speculate on the reasons why the name "anima" was given to the soul. Why was it thought of as feminine? Later I came to see that this inner feminine figure plays a typical, or archetypal, role in the unconscious of a man, and I called her the "anima." The corresponding figure in the unconscious of woman I called the "animus."[26]

Before concluding this important link between Jung's personal individuation process, alchemy, and the anima – his archetypal soul figure – let's pause for a moment to consider its counterpart: the animus. What does a woman's union with her inner masculine half, her soul figure, look like?

In my practice as a psychoanalyst working with women's individuation processes, I have found that the animus, like Jung's anima, is anything but straightforward. It frequently manifests in a woman's relationships with men – whether intimate or professional – often by creating tensions. She may project her inner "wise man" onto a male figure, seeking in him the very nourishment she lacks in relation to her animus. Conversely, she may see him as authoritarian, a patronizing tyrant against whom she feels compelled to compete – outwitting, challenging, or even fighting him in the conviction that she will prevail.

Yet it is worth remembering that the anima and animus form a syzygy – a union of opposites that together create a whole. If one cannot exist without the other, then a woman can indeed develop both – a well-integrated anima, a rich and independent erotic nature, alongside a mature and differentiated animus, her capacity for logos and rational thought.

Lou Andreas-Salomé, who we meet in Chapter Seven, is a remarkable example of such a woman – both industrious and erotic, embodying a rare balance of a fully integrated anima *and* animus.

The chief confidant for Jung during his intense work on alchemy was no doubt Marie-Louise von Franz, who herself wrote and published extensively on alchemical studies, for example, *Alchemical Active Imagination* (1977)[27], *Corpus*

Alchemicum Arabicum (2006))[28], and *Aurora Consurgens: A document attributed to Thomas Aquinas on the problem of opposites in alchemy* (1957).[29]

Synchronicity

Jung lived a rich life demonstrating much of the "inclusive" approach he expounded. Along with embracing metaphysical realms, he remained a scientist, a researcher. In the 1910s and the early years of Albert Einstein's work on relativity, the two men met through their mutual acquaintance, Theodor Flournoy, a Swiss psychologist and professor at the University of Geneva, and struck up a friendship. Jung recounts that he invited Einstein to his home in Küsnacht on multiple occasions for informal discussions. These conversations, especially Einstein's ideas on the relativity of time and space, significantly influenced Jung's thinking, particularly regarding the *psychic reality* and the *relativity of psychic experience*. Jung later admitted that Einstein's revolutionary ideas about the relativity of time and space indirectly led him to consider the idea of synchronicity years later.

Jung defined synchronicity as a principle that connects events in a meaningful way that cannot be explained by causality alone. It suggests an acausal connecting principle underlying certain phenomena, akin to the connections in space-time described by Albert Einstein. While Einstein focused on the interrelationships of physical events in the universe, Jung extended this thinking to the psychological realm, proposing an underlying connection between mind and matter. Just as physical measurements depend on the observer's position, Jung suggested that psychological experiences could also be seen as relative, shaped by the consciousness of the observer.

Jung's memories of Einstein were summarized in a 1953 letter to Carl Selig,

> Professor Einstein was my guest on several occasions at dinner . . . These were very early days when Einstein was developing his first theory of relativity. As non-mathematicians, we psychiatrists had difficulty in following his argument. . . . It was Einstein who first started me off thinking about a possible relativity of time as well as space, and their psychic conditionality. More than thirty years later, this stimulus led to my . . . thesis of psychic synchronicity. . . . One can scarcely imagine a greater contrast than that between the mathematical and the psychological mentality. The one is extremely quantitative and the other is extremely qualitative.[30]

In the 1950s, Jung intensified his exploration of *synchronicity* in collaboration with his friend and former patient, Wolfgang Pauli. A renowned quantum physicist, Pauli had been nominated for the Nobel Prize in Physics by Einstein and won the award in 1945. Pauli shared numerous dreams with Jung, which were rich in symbolic motifs related to physics and cosmic principles. Jung analyzed these as expressions of archetypal content, linking them to his theories on the universal themes of the psyche, alchemy, and archetypes.

Over 20 years of correspondence, Jung and Pauli exchanged ideas on psychology, physics, and philosophy. They explored topics such as archetypes, quantum mechanics, and the nature of reality. Pauli proposed the existence of a *cosmic order of nature* beyond human control, governing both outward material objects and inward images. Together, they developed the *Pauli–Jung Conjecture*, a dual-aspect theory suggesting that mental and physical phenomena are derivative of a shared, psychophysically neutral reality.

Jung and Pauli questioned the adequacy of causality as the sole explanatory principle for all phenomena. They suggested that certain events are connected through meaningful correlations. For instance, when an archetype is activated in the unconscious, it can manifest both psychologically and physically, resulting in synchronistic events. To describe the dimension where psyche and matter intersect, they introduced the concept of the *psychoid*. This term represents a realm that is neither purely psychic nor purely physical but exists at their intersection.

Their collaboration further led to the concept of *unus mundus* or "one world," positing that psyche and matter are two aspects of the same underlying reality. This unified framework resonated with Pauli's quantum theory and Jung's archetypal psychology. They theorized that both psychological and physical phenomena emerge from a shared substrate that unites mind and matter.

Another key area of their collaboration was the role of numbers. They proposed that numbers serve as archetypes that bridge subjective and objective realities, structuring both perception and the physical world. Pauli's belief in a mathematically ordered universe aligned with Jung's view of archetypes shaping consciousness and external phenomena. This shared interest culminated in their co-authored volume *The Interpretation of Nature and the Psyche* (1952), which explored the intersections of psychology and quantum physics.

Pauli's fascination with numbers took on a poignant note during his final days. While hospitalized at the Red Cross Hospital in Zurich in 1958, he was assigned to room number 137. This number had deep significance for Pauli due to its connection with the fine-structure constant in quantum electrodynamics, approximately equal to 1/137. Upon seeing the room number, Pauli reportedly remarked, "I knew it would be 137." He passed away in that room on December 15, 1958, leaving a legacy of collaboration that deeply influenced Jung's work on synchronicity.

Applications of Synchronicity

In *Synchronicity: An Acausal Connecting Principle* (1952), Jung describes how events are linked through synchronicity and shows how such events often reveal deeper layers of the unconscious, mediated by archetypes, which act as bridges between the psyche and external reality.

Jung classified synchronicity into four categories:

1. A psychic state in the observer coincides with a simultaneous acausal event occurring nearby.

2. A psychic state corresponds to an external event occurring outside the observer's immediate perception.
3. A psychic state aligns with a future event distant in time and space.
4. Mantic methods, such as oracles, serve to either produce or reveal synchronistic events.

Let us explore these categories through Jung's notable examples:

Coincidence in Real Time: The Golden Scarab

Jung described treating a young woman who resisted acknowledging unconscious processes. She shared a dream where she received a golden scarab. While recounting this dream, Jung heard a tapping on the window and discovered a rose chafer beetle (*Cetonia aurata*), a type of scarabaeid beetle, attempting to enter. He caught the beetle, handed it to her, and said, "Here is your scarab."

This uncanny coincidence broke through the patient's intellectual defenses, opening her to exploring the unconscious. For Jung, this was a clear example of synchronicity: the external event (the beetle) coincided meaningfully with her psychological state (sharing the dream). He remarked, "This experience punctuated the desired hole in her rationalism and broke the ice of her intellectual resistance. The treatment could now be continued with satisfactory results" (*CW 8*, para. 982).

Correspondence Beyond Immediate Perception: The I Ching Oracle

Jung was fascinated by the *I Ching*, an ancient Chinese system of divination, and frequently used it to explore synchronistic phenomena. On one occasion, he consulted the oracle for a young man with a mother complex who was unsure about marrying a seemingly suitable woman. The hexagram response read: "The maiden is powerful. One should not marry such a maiden." Jung interpreted this synchronistic result as reflecting the archetypal dynamics of the man's conflict, cautioning against a potential repetition of his mother complex.

This example demonstrates how archetypal patterns can manifest beyond immediate perception, revealing the interplay between psyche and external phenomena through mantic methods.

Future Alignment: The Flood Vision

In October 1913, Jung experienced a vivid vision of a catastrophic flood engulfing Europe, followed by rivers of blood. This vision recurred two weeks later with even greater intensity. An inner voice affirmed its reality, stating, "Look at it well; it is wholly real and it will be so. You cannot doubt it." Jung later interpreted this vision as a forewarning of World War I, which began the following year.

For Jung, this vision represented a synchronistic connection between his psychic state and a future collective upheaval, mediated by archetypal imagery.

Mandalas as Archetypes of Synchronicity and the Self

From 1916 onward, Jung adopted the daily practice of drawing mandalas – circular, symbolic images – which he noted as reflections of his evolving inner situation. He observed how these drawings mapped the ongoing transformations of his psyche.

Jung described his mandalas as "cryptograms concerning the state of the self," which he regarded as central to his process of individuation. Over time, these drawings helped him form a living conception of the self, which he described as a monad encompassing wholeness and serving as the microcosm of the psyche. The mandala, he said, represents this monad and corresponds to the microcosmic nature of the psyche.

Through the mandala's symbolic representation, Jung came to recognize the Self as the center and ultimate goal of psychic development. Unlike linear progressions of the psyche, the mandala exemplifies the perpetual recreation and circumambulation of the self.

Synchronistic Confirmation of the Mandala

Jung's recognition of the mandala's universality received profound confirmation in 1928. After painting a mandala he called *Window on Eternity*, depicting a golden, fortified castle at its center, Jung reflected on its uniquely Chinese aesthetic. Soon after, he received a manuscript of the Taoist text *The Secret of the Golden Flower* from his colleague Richard Wilhelm.[31] This Taoist-alchemical treatise confirmed many of Jung's insights about the mandala and the circumambulation of the center. Jung regarded this as a synchronistic moment – an acausal event that deepened his understanding of the collective psyche and its archetypal symbols.

Wilhelm's manuscript further catalyzed Jung's interest in alchemy, leading him to study extensive alchemical literature, beginning with the *Artis Auriferae Volumina Duo* (1593), a seminal collection of Latin treatises on alchemy.

Significance of Synchronicity in Individuation

Jung recognized that synchronicity profoundly impacts the individuation process. These moments demand a release of rigid causality and embrace the paradoxical nature of the psyche. Synchronistic events, united by shared meaning rather than causal links, allow individuals to experience the timeless and eternal quality of the self.

By exploring archetypal images – universally embedded in the psyche – Jung showed how external phenomena could align with internal psychological states to create synchronistic moments. For example, his use of the *I Ching* revealed patterns that helped him uncover future possibilities, showing how synchronicity can illuminate what lies ahead.

Jung remarked, "Synchronicity is no more baffling or mysterious than the discontinuities of physics. It is only the ingrained belief in the sovereign power of causality that creates intellectual difficulties and makes it appear unthinkable that causeless events exist or could ever occur."[32]

Collaborators on Synchronicity

Several of Jung's contemporaries contributed to the development of his ideas on synchronicity, including Barbara Hannah, a close collaborator and biographer of Jung, who incorporated synchronicity into her work. She demonstrated how meaningful coincidences could emerge in dreams and active imagination.

One small example from my own life illustrates such a meaningful coincidence. Long ago, in preparation for my first visit to the tomb of Hazrat Inayat Khan in New Delhi, I found myself contemplating how the experience would be. *Do I need to bring proper water from Holland?. . . Cookies – tick . . . But the toilets, that will be a problem!* My thoughts, initially practical and mundane, gradually deepened into the state of active imagination I had been trained in.

At a certain moment, everything became very still and serene – and suddenly, a huge eagle landed on my right shoulder. I felt the heavy weight of its body, noticed its scent – spicier than my cats, yet still balmy – and what surprised me most was its field of vision: nearly 360 degrees. I had not expected that.

I maintained my practice up until my departure for Delhi. Once there, every morning I performed my Sufi practices in the very tomb of Hazrat Inayat Khan. On my last day, before leaving, I asked the tomb's guardian about the birds that had been circling endlessly above the dome's rooftop. *What are those birds?* I asked.

"Eagles," she answered.

Admittedly, I found this jaw-dropping. Was the "meaningfulness" of this synchronicity simply the realization that such connections exist? In any case, it heightened my awareness of the intricate, unseen dimensions of the world that surround us at all times. I find it endlessly fascinating.

In addition to Wolfgang Pauli, another important figure in Jung's exploration of synchronicity was Victor White, primarily a theological collaborator. His engagement with Jung on the relationship between psychology and spirituality led him to explore themes of acausal meaning, further contributing to Jung's broader framework.

The Numinous: A Mystical Encounter With the Infinite

In 1944, following a broken foot and a heart attack, as we have seen, Carl Gustav Jung experienced a profound series of visions and sensations while teetering on the edge of life and death.

Let us now take a closer look at these experiences, which he later described in his memoirs. They are emblematic of what Rudolf Otto defined as "numinous" – a direct encounter with the *mysterium tremendum et fascinans*, a divine and overwhelming presence that transcends human understanding. For Jung, this was a mystical experience that deeply influenced his psychological and spiritual outlook, reshaping his understanding of the unconscious, the archetypal realm, and the process of individuation – and of himself.

The Vision of the Earth From Space

Jung's journey began with a vivid vision in which he perceived himself high above the earth, gazing down at its luminous, azure beauty. He saw continents, seas, and the shimmering silver outlines of the globe. Specific regions, such as Ceylon and India, came into view, glowing with an otherworldly clarity. The earth appeared alive; a sacred organism imbued with profound significance. This cosmic perspective filled Jung with awe, offering him an unparalleled sense of liberation from the confines of earthly existence.

The earth's radiance and the vastness of the cosmos provided Jung with an overwhelming sense of unity, a profound glimpse into the interconnectedness of life. This vision echoed alchemical and archetypal motifs in his work – the macrocosm mirroring the microcosm. The symbolic nature of this encounter suggested a transcendence of individual ego, aligning with universal archetypes and the collective unconscious.

Jung described the experience as a timeless state, where the usual distinctions of past, present, and future dissolved into an iridescent whole. This was not a product of his imagination but a direct encounter with the eternal – what he called "the ecstasy of a non-temporal state." In this state, he observed existence with complete objectivity, experiencing the unfolding of life as a unity.

Jung recalled the presence of a "pneuma of inexpressible sanctity" that filled his hospital room during the visions. This sanctity, which he likened to the "sweet smell of the Holy Ghost," manifested as the *mysterium coniunctionis*, the alchemical sacred marriage. It symbolized the divine union which Jung embodied during his mystical journey.

The Encounter With the Basileus of Kos

Amid his celestial experience, Jung encountered a figure framed by golden laurel wreaths – his doctor, Dr. H., who appeared in his "primal form" as the *basileus of Kos*, symbolizing wisdom and healing. Jung realized that Dr. H. was an archetypal messenger from the unconscious. In a silent exchange, Dr. H. conveyed a message: Jung was not permitted to leave life yet. This encounter encapsulated the archetype of the healer and prophet, embodying a message from the unconscious that Jung's work on earth was not complete.

The message, and the encounter, was deeply transformative yet laden with disappointment. Jung felt the agony of being pulled back into life, lamenting the need to return to what he perceived as the "box system" of earthly existence – a world fragmented and confined compared to the sublime unity he had experienced.

> I felt violent resistance to my doctor because he had brought me back to life. At the same time, I was worried about him. "His life is in danger, for heaven's sake! He has appeared to me in his primal form! When anybody attains this form it means he is going to die, for already he belongs to the 'greater company'!" Suddenly the terrifying thought came to me that Dr. H. would have to die in my stead. I tried my best to talk to him about it, but he did not understand me. Then I became angry with him. "Why does he always pretend he doesn't know he is a basileus of Kos? And that he has already assumed his primal form? He wants to make me believe that he doesn't know!" That irritated me. . . ."Damn it all, he ought to watch his step. He has no right to be so reckless! I want to tell him to take care of himself." I was firmly convinced that his life was in jeopardy.[33]

In actual fact, Jung was his last patient. On April 4, 1944, Dr. H. took to his bed and did not leave it again. He died of septicemia. Jung felt Dr. H. was a good doctor and that there was something of the genius about him. Otherwise, he would not have appeared to him as a prince of Kos, he concluded.

Mystical Imagery: The Garden of Pomegranates and the Hieros Gamos

As Jung lingered between life and death, his visions transformed into symbolic representations of mystical union and divine marriage. He found himself in the *Pardes Rimmonim* – the Garden of Pomegranates, a symbol drawn from Kabbalistic traditions. Here, the wedding of Tifereth (beauty) and Malchuth (kingdom), representing the union of male and female principles within the divine, took place. Jung felt he was not just an observer but the marriage itself, a living embodiment of the *coniunctio* – the alchemical merging of opposites into wholeness.

The imagery shifted to the Marriage of the Lamb in a celestial Jerusalem, followed by the hieros gamos of Zeus and Hera in a classical amphitheater. These archetypal unions symbolized cosmic harmony and the integration of the psyche. For Jung, they underscored the central role of the Self as the unifying principle in the individuation process.

In his later reflections on true *coniunctio*, Jung writes,

> after the death of my wife. I saw her in a dream which was like a vision. She stood at some distance from me, looking at me squarely. She was in her prime, perhaps about thirty, and wearing the dress which had been made for her many years before by my cousin the medium. It was perhaps the most beautiful thing she had ever worn. Her expression was neither joyful nor sad, but, rather,

objectively wise and understanding, without the slightest emotional reaction, as though she were beyond the mist of affects. I knew that it was not she, but a portrait she had made or commissioned for me. It contained the beginning of our relationship, the events of fifty-three years of marriage, and the end of her life also. Face to face with such wholeness one remains speechless, for it can scarcely be comprehended.

The objectivity which I experienced in this dream and in the visions is part of a completed individuation. It signifies detachment from valuations and from what we call emotional ties. In general, emotional ties are very important to human beings. But they still contain projections, and it is essential to withdraw these projections in order to attain to oneself and to objectivity. Emotional relationships are relationships of desire, tainted by coercion and constraint; something is expected from the other person, and that makes him and ourselves unfree. Objective cognition lies hidden behind the attraction of the emotional relationship; it seems to be the central secret. Only through objective cognition is the real coniunctio possible.[34]

The Struggle to Return

After his celestial journey, Jung struggled to reconcile the numinous experiences with the mundane reality of earthly life. The world seemed artificial, like a tattered stage set. He resented being "tethered" back to the material realm, perceiving it as a prison compared to the freedom of the eternal, timeless state he had experienced. He described the transition as a painful process of reentry, akin to re-assuming a burdensome identity after shedding it. This stark contrast between the numinous unity of his visions and the fragmented reality of daily life underscored the tension between the eternal and the temporal, a theme central to his work on individuation.

Despite his resistance, Jung eventually found affirmation in his return to life. This experience deepened his resolve to accept existence as it is, including its limitations and contradictions. For Jung, this marked an "unconditional 'yes' to that which is," a profound acceptance of fate and the path of individuation.

Impact on Consciousness and Legacy

More than once, I have heard from individuals who have had near-death experiences that returning to life is not a moment of relief, but a struggle – often hard and painful. I believe that's why they come to me.

I once attended a seminar led by Pim van Lommel, a Dutch cardiologist who has conducted extensive research on near-death experiences, particularly their long-term impact. What stood out most was not just the experience itself, but how it profoundly transformed the lives of those who underwent it. His research[35] shows that survivors develop a heightened intuitive sensitivity, a deeper appreciation for life, increased compassion for others, and a diminished fear of death – enduring shifts in perception and behavior.

Likewise, through my conversations with those who come to my practice, I have sensed that the numinous encounter at the heart of a near-death experience profoundly reorients a person's understanding of life, death, and consciousness itself.

Jung's own near-death experience provided him with a direct encounter with the archetypal dimensions of existence, reinforcing his belief in the interconnectedness of psyche and cosmos. The visions offered a confirmation of his ideas on the collective unconscious and the archetypes, particularly the Self as the central integrative force of the psyche. The experience also solidified his understanding of the *mysterium coniunctionis*, the alchemical process of uniting opposites, which became a cornerstone of his later work.

Jung's encounter with death and the hereafter had a lasting impact on his creativity and productivity. Following his recovery, he entered one of the most fruitful periods of his career, writing some of his most important works. The visions also deepened his spiritual perspective, leading him to explore questions of life, death, and the afterlife with renewed vigor. Jung saw these experiences as affirmations of a greater cosmic order, a mysterious unity underpinning existence.

Jung's numinous near-death experience was a profound moment of psychological and spiritual awakening. It revealed to him the depths of the unconscious and the archetypal patterns that shape human existence. Through his visions, Jung faced the eternal, timeless essence of life, a state of wholeness that transcends the divided nature of ordinary reality. This experience enriched his understanding of the psyche and reaffirmed his commitment to the individuation process as a path to integrate the opposites and realize the Self.

For Jung, his numinous visions served as a lived myth – a symbolic enactment of death and rebirth. This mythic dimension of his near-death experience provided a profound affirmation of his psychological theories, where myths and archetypes serve as bridges to the unconscious, guiding individuals through transformative thresholds.

Notes

1 Carl G. Jung, *The Red Book: Liber Novus: A Reader's Edition,* ed. Sonu Shamdasani (New York: W. W. Norton, 2009); *Opening page* (Signed C. G. Jung, 1957).
2 Jung's publications prior to 1913, apart from the aforementioned *Psychology of the Unconscious* consist of his doctoral thesis *On the Psychology and Pathology of So-Called Occult Phenomena* (1902), *Studies in Word Association* (1906) Co-authored with Franz Riklin, this work documented his early research on complexes through word association tests. *The Content of the Psychoses* (1908), a study on psychotic phenomena, incorporating concepts related to unconscious processes, and, *The Psychology of Dementia Praecox* (1907), are major works on schizophrenia (then called dementia praecox), influencing his theories on the unconscious.
3 Carl G. Jung, *Memories, Dreams, Reflections*, ed. Aniela Jaffé, trans. Richard and Clara Winston (New York: Vintage, 1989), 179.
4 Jung, *Memories, Dreams, Reflections*, 188–189.
5 Carl G. Jung, *The Red Book: Liber Novus: A Reader's Edition,* ed. Sonu Shamdasani (New York: W. W. Norton, 2009), 142–144.
6 Jung, *The Red Book*, 237.

7   Jung, *Memories, Dreams, Reflections*, 222.
8   See, *Synchronicity: An Acausal Connecting Principle*, first published in 1952. In this work, he defines synchronicity as the occurrence of events that are meaningfully related yet lack a direct causal connection. These events coincide in time and appear significantly related, even though there is no identifiable cause-and-effect link between them. See also the section titled Synchronicity in this chapter.
9   Jung, *Memories, Dreams, Reflections*, 183.
10 Jung, *The Red Book: Liber Novus: A Reader's Edition*, 183.
11 Jung, *The Red Book: Liber Novus: A Reader's Edition*, 511.
12 C. G. Jung, *The Black Books 1913–1932: Notebooks of Transformation*, ed. Sonu Shamdasani, trans. Martin Liebscher, John Peck, and Sonu Shamdasani (New York: W. W. Norton & Company, 2020), 17–18.
13 Jung, *Memories, Dreams, Reflections*, 174.
14 Catrine Clay, *Labyrinths: Emma Jung, Her Marriage to Carl, and the Early Years of Psychoanalysis* (New York: Harper, 2016).
15 Jung, *The Red Book: Liber Novus: A Reader's Edition*, 174–176.
16 Jung, *Memories, Dreams, Reflections*, 181.
17 Jung, *The Red Book: Liber Novus: A Reader's Edition*, 177.
18 Jung, *The Red Book: Liber Novus: A Reader's Edition*, 179–180.
19 In *Aion*, Jung noted that serpents were a typical pair of opposites, and that the conflict between serpents was a motif found in medieval alchemy. Carl Gustav Jung, Aion: Researches into the Phenomenology of the Self. Collected Works of C. G. Jung, 9 vols, no. 2, 181 (1951).
20 Jung, *The Red Book: Liber Novus: A Reader's Edition*, 189.
21 Jung, *The Red Book: Liber Novus: A Reader's Edition*, 17.
22 Jung, *Psychological Types, Collected Works of C. G. Jung*, 6 vol. (Princeton, NJ: Princeton University Press, 1971 [1921]).
23 Toni Wolff, *Structural Forms of the Feminine Psyche* (Zurich: Students Association, C.G. Jung Institute, 1956), 7.
24 Jung, *Memories, Dreams, Reflections*, 187–188.
25 Jung, *Memories, Dreams, Reflections*, 209.
26 Jung, *Memories, Dreams, Reflections*, 186.
27 A psychological interpretation of alchemical imagery through active imagination, connecting medieval symbolism with Jungian analysis.
28 Von Franz's analysis of a key alchemical manuscript traditionally linked to Thomas Aquinas, examining alchemy's symbolism of opposites and individuation.
29 Provides von Franz's psychological commentary on *Hall ar-Rumuz*, a work attributed to Ibn Umail, bridging Arabic alchemical tradition with Jungian interpretation.
30 Jung, *Carl Jung, Letters Vol. II*, ed. Aniela Jaffé (Princeton, NJ: Princeton University Press, 1974), 108–109.
31 Jung, *The Secret of the Golden Flower: A Chinese Book of Life*, trans. Richard Wilhelm, commentary by C. G. Jung (London: Routledge & Kegan Paul, 1931).
32 Jung, *The Structure and Dynamics of the Psyche, Vol. 8 of the Collected Works of C.G. Jung*, ed. R. F. C. Hull (Princeton, NJ: Princeton University Press, 1969), 518.
33 Jung, *Memories, Dreams, Reflections*, 293.
34 Jung, *Memories, Dreams, Reflections*, 296–297.
35 Pim van Lommel, *Consciousness Beyond Life: The Science of the Near-Death Experience* (New York: Harper Collins Publishers, 2011).

Chapter 5

Hazrat Inayat Khan

Biography and Main Life Events

For Inayat Khan, the path to self-knowledge reached far beyond names, appearances, or character traits. To truly know oneself was to stand before the mystery of one's own existence – to sense, both in thought and in lived experience, the deeper questions that call from within: Where have I come from? For what purpose was I born? How long is my stay upon this earth, and of what am I really made? To seek self-realization, in his understanding, was to uncover the hidden composition of one's being and to awaken to the unique purpose held within the soul, the very purpose by which it was drawn into this world.

Early Life and Roots

Hazrat Inayat Khan, the renowned 20th-century Sufi mystic, musician, and teacher, was born on July 5, 1882, in Baroda, India, into a family where music and mysticism formed the very foundation of life. The home of his maternal grandfather, Maula Bakhsh, was a patriarchal household alive with harmony, discipline, and deep cultural devotion. Though a grand household of 30 to 40 relatives, it was the women of the family – his great-aunt, grandmother, and mother – who brought a quiet strength and grace, each holding a vital role in maintaining the order and spirit of the home.

Inayat Khan's father, Mashaik Rahmat Khan, hailed from a lineage of mystics and musicians in the Punjab. A master of the classical dhrupad tradition, Rahmat Khan had journeyed from his ancestral lands to serve as a court musician in Baroda. His artistry and ascetic roots deeply influenced the young Inayat, blending the external beauty of sound with the internal search for divine truth. His mother, Khatidja Bibi, the learned second daughter of Maula Bakhsh, was well versed in Arabic, Persian, and Urdu. Inayat Khan would later reflect upon the profound spiritual bond he shared with her – an unspoken connection of love that transcended space and time. This bond would manifest in moments of intuition and shared dreams, a harbinger of his later understanding of spiritual unity.

At the heart of his formative years was his grandfather, Maula Bakhsh (1833–1896), a towering figure in Indian music who earned reverence across the land. A man of genius and innovation, Maula Bakhsh had unified diverse musical

DOI: 10.4324/9781003431336-5

Figure 5.1 Hazrat Inayat Khan.

traditions through a groundbreaking system of notation. He devoted his life to the Gayanshala, India's first academy of music, where he shaped not only musicians but a cultural renaissance. The young Inayat absorbed the rhythms and philosophy of music under his grandfather's guidance, and it was here, in the halls of the Gayanshala, that he first learned to see music as more than an art – it was the voice of the divine, a bridge to the infinite. Naturally, Maula Bakhsh's musical passion and reputation had a significant impact on Inayat Khan, who received a thorough grounding in the philosophy, theory, and practice of music. Inayat Khan sought perfection in and through music. He also showed curiosity and admiration for the West, to which Maula Bakhsh's younger son, Alaoddin Khan, who had studied Western music in England at the Royal Academy and the Royal College of Music, later introduced him.

When Inayat Khan, at the age of 9, turned to his grandfather for consolation in a moment of spiritual despair, feeling his prayers were not heard, Maula Bakhsh quietly responded with words that would forever alter his grandson's life: "The signs of God are seen in the world, and the world is seen in thyself." Inayat Khan later recalled how these words pierced his soul like a shaft of light, awakening in him a vision of divine immanence. From that moment, every breath of nature, every note of music, became for him a reflection of the Divine Presence.

These words entered so deeply into my spirit, that from this time every moment of my life has been occupied with the thought of the divine immanence; and my eyes were thus opened, as the eyes of the young man by Elijah, to see the symbols of God in all the aspects of nature, and also in that nature which is reflected within myself. This sudden illumination made everything appear as clear to me as in a crystal bowl or a translucent jewel. Thenceforth I devoted myself to the absorption and attainment of truth, the immortal and perfected Grace.[1]

This illumination shaped his lifelong path – one that merged the external quest for beauty with the inward journey toward Truth.

Education and Early Influences

Baroda, at the turn of the 19th century, was a place of transition, where the traditions of India intersected with the modernizing influences of British colonial rule. Though born into a Muslim family, Inayat Khan attended a Marathi (Hindu) school, where his artistic and poetic gifts often went unnoticed. To his teachers, he seemed distracted, a dreamer more attuned to unseen worlds than the rigid calculations of arithmetic. His poetic leanings, too, were frowned upon. Even his father sought to dissuade him, warning that withdrawal into solitude would lead only to isolation. "To think deeply and to live for others," Rahmat Khan once told him, "is greater than a life of reclusion, for loving others is loving God." These words planted within Inayat Khan a seed of wisdom that would blossom years later, shaping his emphasis on selfless service.

Turning 17: Teachers and Travels

At the age of 17, Inayat Khan experienced a profound loss with the passing of his mother, an event that marked the beginning of a period of deep inward searching. By 1902, he left Baroda and began a series of travels through India, immersing himself in its sacred traditions and meeting mystics, saints, and scholars. His first travel was to Madras, and then on to Mysore and later to Bombay, today known as Mumbai, then reaching Hyderabad aged 21.

In Hyderabad, at the age of 21, he composed the *Minqar-i Musiqar*, a monumental work in Urdu and Persian that treated Hindustani music as a sacred science, bridging art and mysticism. It was here, too, that his music brought him before the Nizam (sovereign ruler) of Hyderabad, who bestowed upon him the title *Tansen az-Zaman* – the Tansen of the Age – acknowledging his unparalleled mastery.

When asked to reveal the secret of his music, Inayat Khan replied:

As sound is the highest source of manifestation it is mysterious itself. And whosoever has the knowledge of sound, he indeed knows the secret of the universe. My music is my thought and my thought is my emotion. The deeper I dive into the ocean of feeling, the more beautiful are the pearls I bring forth in the forms of melodies. Thus my music creates feelings within me even before others feel it. My music is my religion, therefore worldly success can never be a fit price for it and my sole object in music is to achieve perfection.[2]

Encounter With the Murshid

In Hyderabad, destiny brought Inayat Khan to his spiritual guide, Sayyed Abu Hashim Madani, a saint and scholar of the Chishti Order, steeped in the traditions of Ibn Arabi. Madani's teachings were gentle and profound, delivered not through formal instruction but through presence and metaphor. Where others might speak of doctrines, Madani pointed to the trees, the rivers, and the wind – signs of God's unity manifest in creation.

Let us now, in the context of Inayat Khan's Sufi training, touch upon Ibn Arabi's work which so influenced Madani and in turn Inayat Khan. Ibn al-Arabi (1165–1240) is considered one of the most influential mystics in the history of Sufism and Islamic philosophy. He was born in the region of Al-Andalus, Spain, and grew up in a highly intellectual and spiritually inclined family, which from an early age offered him a thorough education in various fields, including Islamic jurisprudence, studies of the Qur'an, and the Hadith, paired with deep intellectual conversations with eminent scholars.

At the age of 16, Ibn Arabi had a transformative spiritual experience known as his "First Illumination," in which he claimed to have received direct knowledge and spiritual insights from God. This experience became a turning point in his life and marked the beginning of his mystical journey and later writings. During his subsequent training and mystical development, Ibn al-Arabi created a unique (and complex) philosophical and mystical system outlining the very notion of "Unity of Being," *Wahdat al-Wujud*, in which God is the sole reality and hence all of creation is a manifestation, reflection, and expression of the divine. Ibn Arabi established the concept of "Perfect Man" (*insan al-kamil*) to identify the self-realized human being, representing a microcosm of the entire cosmos and embodying the divine attributes to the fullest extent. His teachings are exemplary studies of *Wahdat al-Wujud*. In one of his poems we read, "Love is the creed I hold: wherever turns His camels, Love is still my creed and faith."

It is an interesting synchronicity that Inayat Khan, aged around 12, had a similarly enlightening experience. Through his grandfather's words, "The signs of God are seen in the world and the world is seen in thyself," he experienced his own instant realization of divine immanence.

Under Abu Hashim Madani's guidance, Inayat Khan experienced a deep spiritual penetration, absorbing the teachings of divine immanence and the unity of being.

Abu Hashim Madani recognized the luminous soul before him and bestowed upon Inayat Khan his spiritual transmission, entrusting him with a sacred mission: to carry the wisdom of Sufism to the West. "May God strengthen your faith," Madani blessed him, a simple but potent prayer that became Inayat Khan's anchor in the years ahead.

When Madani passed in 1907, Inayat Khan was stricken with grief. Yet, he understood that his Murshid lived on in all forms of beauty and holiness. He set out on a pilgrimage through India, seeking glimpses of his teacher's presence in the faces of saints and sages. This journey deepened his resolve, for he knew that his calling was not to remain in the East but to carry the flame of Truth to lands yet untouched by the Sufism he knew so well.

Hazrat Inayat Khan's Journey of the Sufi Message

By 1910, Inayat Khan had established himself as one of India's most celebrated musicians, revered not only for his art but for the spiritual depths it conveyed. Yet, when the moment came, he left it all behind – his career, his reputation, and his homeland – to follow the vision that had been revealed to him. In his own words, "I was transported by destiny from the world of lyric and poetry to the world of industry and commerce."

Thus, on September 13, 1910, Hazrat Inayat Khan boarded a ship bound for America, accompanied by his two brothers, Maheboob Khan (1887–1948) and Musharaff Khan (1895–1967), and his cousin Mohammed Ali Khan (1881–1958).

As the waves rose and fell beneath him, he gazed upon the vast ocean and saw in its rhythm the rise and fall of life itself. His heart, however, remained steady, guided by the divine voice that reassured him: "Thou art sent on Our service, and it is We Who will make thy way clear."[3]

This marked the beginning of a journey that would take him across continents, through trials and triumphs, as he carried a message of divine unity to a world ready to awaken. It was not only a journey of geography but a passage of transformation – for himself, for those he touched, and for the countless souls who would come to hear the music of his words long after his physical passage had ended.

The Call to the West (1912–1915)

Between 1912 and 1915, Hazrat Inayat Khan traveled extensively through France, Russia, and the United Kingdom. He considered these years a time of learning rather than teaching, as he faced numerous challenges adapting to Western culture, lifestyle, and philosophy. He identified three main difficulties during this period: cultural differences, the loss of his music, and financial struggles.

Cultural Differences

Inayat Khan observed profound differences between Eastern and Western thought, which often left him feeling alienated. He remarked:

> The man in the Western world, who cannot stand even a king over his head, naturally rebels against a God to be considered as an Emperor of emperors. The modern man does not want anyone to be superior to himself; a priest, savior, or God, none of them he cares for. If there is anything that appeals to him, it is to know of the divine character to be found in the innermost nature of man. The man today is absolutely against a spiritual hierarchy and therefore naturally against the head of the hierarchy, who is God.[4]

This insight helped him shape his teachings for Western audiences, focusing more on the immanence of the divine within individuals rather than traditional hierarchies.

Loss of Music

Music had been the lifeblood of Inayat Khan's spiritual journey and personal identity. However, his demanding travels made it impossible to maintain regular practice. Reflecting on this loss, he wrote:

> There came a time when I could not have sufficient time to keep up my musical practice, which was too great a loss for my heart to sustain. Yet I had to bear it, for every moment of my time was absorbed in the work. I especially yearned for the music of India, the fluid with which my soul was nourished from the moment I was born on earth. But for my music, the soil of India was necessary, the juice of that soil for me to live on, the air of India to breathe, the sky of India to look at, and the sun of India to be inspired by.[5]

Financial Struggles

Financial hardship was another significant challenge during this period. When traveling through Russia, he and his brothers informed their family in Baroda to stop their monthly allowances, expecting to return to India soon. However, the outbreak of World War I disrupted their plans, forcing them to stay in Britain without sufficient means. Inayat Khan reflected on this period of poverty:

> Poverty proved to be my bitterest enemy. For it always put me in a position that gave my adversaries every facility they desired to cause me harm. With all my mistakes and failings, which I must not disown, I have always tried to avoid dishonor. I was several times in a position which I should never have chosen to be in, but I was constrained by unfortunate circumstances. My pride at the time was very much hurt, and often that happened. If there are any pages in the book of my life which I would rather be closed than open, they are the narrative of my lack of means.[6]

America (1910–1912)

Hazrat Inayat Khan left India for America in September 1910. As the ship approached New York, he gazed at the Statue of Liberty, reflecting on its symbolic promise of freedom. He pondered how the message of spiritual liberty he bore could transform from mere material aspirations to the deeper, spiritual liberty that all humanity seeks.

Arriving in a city bustling with industry and innovation, he found himself in a world vastly different from India. The frenetic pace of New York, with its towering buildings, subway systems, and ceaseless energy, was both alien and fascinating. The message he carried – focused on unity and divine love – needed a medium of communication that would resonate with this new audience. Music, his lifelong passion and mastery, became the bridge.

Through the support of key individuals, such as Professor Cornelius Reebner at Columbia University and Ruth St. Denis, Inayat Khan began to introduce Indian music as a spiritual art form. Yet, he quickly realized that for most Americans, this music was entertainment rather than a profound expression of divine beauty. Despite this challenge, his lectures and performances planted the seeds of interest in Eastern mysticism. Most significantly, in San Francisco, he initiated his first American disciple, Mrs. Ada Martin, who would become Murshida Rabia and dedicate her life to Inayat Khan's Sufi Message.

England (1912–1913)

In England, Hazrat Inayat Khan encountered a culture steeped in tradition and formality. He was introduced to musicians and intellectuals, such as Cecil Scott and Percy Grainger, who took an interest in his art. At literary gatherings, he met prominent figures like Rabindranath Tagore and Lord Dunsany, who appreciated his insights into Sufi poetry.

However, he found the English audience more resistant to the spiritual dimensions of his music. During this period, he began to discern the broader challenges of introducing his Sufi Message to the West. Many in England, skeptical of organized religion and bound by rationalism, resisted the God-ideal. Hazrat Inayat Khan noted a widespread rejection of hierarchical spiritual authority, an attitude that would shape how he presented the teachings moving forward.

In London, 1913, Inayat Khan married Ora Ray Baker, henceforth entitled Begum, whom he had met a year earlier in America. Ora, born in New Mexico in 1892, was captivated by Inayat Khan from their first meeting, drawn to his music and spiritual presence. After their initial encounter, she began writing to him daily, seeking a deeper connection. However, her half-brother, who was her guardian, opposed their union, delaying contact for a significant period, apparently for racist reasons.

Despite these challenges, Ora and Inayat Khan's union became a cornerstone of his life. Together, they had four children within five years, between 1914 and 1919. Inayat Khan spoke of Ora as a faithful and selfless companion who endured the trials of his mission with grace and resilience.

The tests that my life was destined to go through were not of a usual character, and were not a small trial for her. A life such as mine, which was wholly devoted to the Cause, and which was more and more involved in the ever-growing activities of the Sufi Movement, naturally kept me back from that thought and attention which was due to my home and family. Most of the time of my life I was obliged to spend out of home, and when at home, I have always been full of activities, and it naturally fell upon her always to welcome guests with a smile under all circumstances. If I had not been helped by her, my life, laden with a heavy responsibility, would have never enabled me to devote myself entirely to the Order as I have. It is by this continual sacrifice that she has shown her devotion to the Cause.[7]

Ora's role extended far beyond the domestic sphere; her steadfastness allowed Inayat Khan to focus fully on his mission.

France (1913)

In Paris, the cultural epicenter of Europe, Hazrat Inayat Khan found an audience more open to the artistic and mystical dimensions of his work. Collaborating with Edmond Bailly and other notable figures, he performed and lectured on Indian music, captivating luminaries such as composer Claude Debussy. Debussy, deeply moved by the spiritual depth of Indian ragas, referred to his experience as "an evening of emotions."

The intellectual climate of France, with its disillusionment toward institutional religion, posed a unique challenge. At the same time, *A Sufi Message of Spiritual Liberty*, as yet in manuscript form, was translated by Mlle. Jorys, and the French translation published afterwards by Monsieur Bailly. Inayat Khan sought to frame his teachings in a way that would resonate with the French emphasis on individual spirituality and artistic expression. His connections with poets and philosophers like Jules Bois and Isadora Duncan reinforced his understanding of how art could serve as a medium for spiritual awakening.

Russia (1913–1914)

Hazrat Inayat Khan's time in Russia revealed a land of contrasts. Amid the grandeur of imperial culture and the warmth of its people, he sensed an undercurrent of unrest. His lectures at institutions such as the Imperial Conservatory of Music drew enthusiastic audiences, including notable artists like composer Alexander Scriabin.

In Russia, he met philosophers and mystics whose curiosity about Eastern spirituality provided fertile ground for the Message. He noted their depth of questioning, their yearning for meaning, and their reverence for art and beauty. Yet, he also saw in their material excesses and political tensions the signs of an impending upheaval, a premonition that would later be realized in the Russian Revolution.

England (1914–1920)

Returning to England during World War I, Inayat Khan faced an audience consumed by the war's chaos. Calls for peace and spiritual unity were met with skepticism and, at times, hostility. Despite the challenges, he persevered, forming a modest circle of disciples and publishing works such as *The Way of Illumination*.

The war years tested his resolve, but they also deepened his understanding of humanity's struggles. His English disciples, particularly Miss Mary Williams and Miss Lucy Goodenough, played pivotal roles in sustaining the nascent Sufi Order during this difficult period.

Holland (1921)

In Holland, Inayat Khan found a more receptive audience. The Dutch people, known for their pragmatism and openness, embraced his teachings with enthusiasm. Collaborations with figures like Baron van Tuyll van Serooskerken helped establish a thriving Sufi community, with branches in The Hague, Amsterdam, and Arnhem.

The Dutch interest in systematic organization and spiritual ideals provided a supportive environment for the growth of the Sufi Order. Inayat Khan recognized in Holland a nation poised to contribute meaningfully to the spread of the Sufi Message.

America (1923)

When Inayat Khan returned to America in 1923, he encountered a nation still grappling with racial prejudice and materialism. Yet, he also saw in its diversity and dynamism a profound potential for the Message of unity. His detention at Ellis Island due to immigration quotas underscored the challenges of a world divided by borders and biases.

Once again, Mrs. Ada Martin played a central role in facilitating his mission, organizing events and introducing him to new audiences. Inayat Khan's lectures and personal encounters during this second American journey further established the foundations for the Sufi Order in the West.

Organization

While Hazrat Inayat Khan did not initially set out to create an organization, one inevitably arose as a response to the needs of his devoted *mureeds* (disciples), who sought to formalize their connection to his teachings. Addressing the tension between those who supported and those who opposed such structure, Inayat Khan observed in 1922:

> Often a question has been asked of me by many enthusiastic and devoted *mureeds* wishing to work to help further the cause: In what manner are we to set to work? Some thought that a good organization or a firm basis would be necessary; others thought, on the contrary, that in spiritual work, organization was not necessary at all – it spoils its sacredness and gives that which is spiritual a worldly flavor. It has been a very great difficulty to reconcile these two contrary ideas.[8]

Despite initial hesitations, Inayat recognized the need for an organizational vessel to ensure the continuity of his teachings. He supported the establishment of the Sufi Order in London in 1915, and later, in 1922, the Sufi Movement found a new administrative base in Geneva, Switzerland. Collaborators such as Monsieur de Cruzat Zanetti, Monsieur Talewar Dussaq, and his sister, Comtesse M. L. Pieri, brought efficiency and dedication to the organization, ensuring its sustainability. Inayat Khan often used metaphors to illustrate this necessity, likening an organization to a ship needed to cross the sea or a basket for gathering flowers. In 1926, he elaborated: "Every institution and every activity that is intended to do some spiritual work cannot exist without a form. The form is as necessary as it is for human beings to have four walls and a roof."

The Objectives of the Sufi Order

The initial objectives of the Sufi Order were clearly defined:

1. To establish a human brotherhood that transcends considerations of caste, creed, race, nation, or religion, recognizing that differences are the root of discord and suffering.

2. To spread the wisdom of the Sufis, which, although a hidden treasure, is the shared heritage of all humanity and belongs to no single race or religion.
3. To make mysticism accessible, dispelling the mystery and ignorance surrounding it while guiding believers to sincerity and disbelievers to understanding.
4. To harmonize the East and West through music, the universal language, by fostering an exchange of knowledge and reviving unity.
5. To produce Sufi literature that offers profound beauty and instruction across all aspects of knowledge.

Among these objectives, the emphasis on a classless and inclusive vision extended to gender equality – a progressive stance rooted in Inayat Khan's upbringing and central to his work.

Women in the Sufi Order

Inayat Khan recognized the universal feminine principle as integral to spirituality and societal harmony. He viewed balance as essential in spiritual development, promoting the integration of masculine and feminine qualities both within individuals and in the world. The nurturing, intuitive, and compassionate dimensions of the feminine principle, he believed, were vital for personal and collective transformation.

> I see as clear as daylight that the hour is coming when woman will lead humanity to a higher evolution.[9]

He not only affirmed the spiritual role of women but actively involved them in his teachings and organizational efforts. Women participated equally in mixed-gender gatherings, but their contributions went beyond participation – they became central to the growth of the Sufi Order.

Inayat Khan encouraged women to cultivate their intellectual, artistic, and spiritual capacities, and it was often women who meticulously documented his teachings. Dutch *mureed* and artist Saida van Tuyll van Serooskerken recounted one such moment during the first Summer School in 1921:

> Murshid said to me, 'This summer . . . I will dictate to you a book on Greek symbolism, a book on Egyptian symbolism, a book on Assyrian symbolism, and a book on the psychology of Persian poetry and a book on the art of dance.' Well, I thought, that's too much; each one of those books is a life's work! But I didn't dare say this. That is why I asked, 'And Murshid, where shall we start?' 'With Greek symbolism,' he replied.[10]

Through their work, women became vital custodians of his teachings, ensuring their preservation and dissemination.

Pioneering Women of the Early 20th-Century Sufi Order

Several women played pivotal roles in the Sufi Order, receiving initiations and serving as cornerstones of the organization. Among them were

Rabia Martin
Sharifa Goodenough
Sophia Saintsbury-Green
Fazal Mai Egeling
Nargis Dowland
Saida van Tuyll van Serooskerken
Nekbakht Furnée
Kismet Stam

Sharifa Goodenough, appointed by Inayat Khan as Madar-ul-Maham, Silsele-ye Sufiyan, Secretary of the Esoteric School, became instrumental in organizational work. Sophia Saintsbury-Green was particularly active in the Universal Worship and was the first person ordained as a Cheraga (conductor of the Universal Worship ceremony) by Inayat Khan.

Figure 5.2 Hazrat Inayat Khan with family members and mureeds, London 1918.

Despite challenges, including the resistance of some male collaborators, Inayat Khan praised the contributions of women:

> Among some of my male collaborators, I saw a spirit of slight contempt towards the women workers. Nevertheless, however much qualified men proved to be in the work, the valuable service that women have rendered to the cause has been incomparably greater.[11]

Through his teachings and actions, Inayat Khan laid the foundation for a balanced spiritual community, affirming the equality and significance of all participants, regardless of gender. His recognition of women's roles – both spiritual and organizational – remains a defining legacy of his Sufism.

Hierarchy Versus Democracy

Inayat Khan's teachings, rooted in the *murshid–mureed* (guide-disciple) relationship, emphasized the hierarchical transmission of spiritual knowledge through a chain of initiates.

The idea behind this is that of a *silsila*, where the teachings are conveyed through a chain of initiates who have all essentially taught the same wisdom. Ibn Arabi, an initiate in the Qadiri *Silsila,* was perhaps the most important influence on Murshid Madani, although Madani transmitted four lineages: Chishti, Qadiri, Suhrawardi, and Naqshbandi. Madani's guidance and influence upon Inayat was, as we have seen, primarily of the Chishti *Silsila,* in which the chief principle is *Wahdat al-Wujud.* This kind of knowledge is not readily available through books or private meditations. It takes transmission through guidance. It is key to both leadership and discipleship. Yet guidance remains a hierarchical notion, stressing the importance of service, discipleship, and the ongoing annihilation of the ego as prerequisites for the guidance process.[12]

Nevertheless, it was Westerners, educated in a Christian tradition – whether theosophy, Protestantism, Catholicism, or other – and along the more analytic, rationalist, individualist, and democratic principles developed in 19th-century science and philosophy, who comprised the majority of followers and carried out the organizational work. So, although impressed and inspired by Hazrat Inayat Khan's mysticism and guidance, those who played a central role in organizational matters tended to follow a democratic system based on the rule of the majority, in which lobbying and politics could be used for acquiring important roles and responsibilities.[13]

The contrast between an inner process of gradual annihilation of the ego and surrender to God, and individual self-expression in the organizational context, gradually polarized the organization into many facets.

The Crisis of 1925

Tensions came to a head in 1925 when two prominent *mureeds* proposed a formal separation between the Esoteric School, to be led by Inayat Khan, and the exoteric legal body, International Headquarters, to be managed by officials. This proposal also sought to abolish Inayat Khan's plural voting rights.

Although the majority of National Representatives voted in favor, Inayat Khan vetoed the motion, feeling deeply betrayed.

This crisis, coupled with increasing health issues, marked a period of great disappointment for him.

After the Summer School in 1925, Inayat Khan returned to America and visited multiple locations including San Francisco, Oakland, Berkeley, Beverly Hills, Santa Barbara, Los Angeles, San Diego, and Pasadena, where he offered lectures and met with *mureeds*.

I found my work in the West the most difficult task that I could have ever imagined. To work in the West for a spiritual cause to me was like travelling in a hilly land, not like sailing in the sea, which is smooth and level. In the first place I was not a missionary of a certain faith, delegated to the West by its adherents, nor was I sent to the West as a representative of Eastern cult by some Maharaja. I came to the West with His message, whose call I had received, and there was nothing earthly to back me in my mission, except my faith in God and trust in Truth.[14]

Then later, on 28 September 1926, after the last Summer School in Sureness, he traveled back to India via Egypt, Karachi, and on to Lahore, New Delhi, Agra, Benares, Ajmer, Jaipur, and Baroda together with his secretary Kismet Stam. In a lecture at Delhi University, he addressed his concern related to polarization between Muslim and Hindu communities and suggested manners of bridging those through music.

When in Delhi, he went for his regular evening walks:

Darkness came soon after sunset. That is why one could nearly not see the river; one only could hear the soft rippling of its waters. Long times Murshid stood before the black stream. At the other side thousands of jackals were howling in the wilderness. Then Murshid went home in silence.[15]

Hazrat Inayat Khan passed away in the south-room of Tilak Lodge, Daya Lane, on Saturday, 5 February 1927, at 8:20 in the morning, aged 44. There was a storm the night before he passed away.

Inayat Khan's Sufism: Key Philosophical Concepts and Teachings

Inayat Khan, trained by and devoted to Abu Hashim Madani, who in turn was an Ibn Arabi scholar, naturally upheld and repeated the principles of the Sufism he was taught and trained in. Yet, as is common in mystical orders, he molded those into an amalgamation we now know as *The Sufi Message*. In this sense, it was formed by his unorthodox personality, musical upbringing and education, mystical training in the Chishti and other earlier mentioned Sufi orders, his personal Samadhi realization, and his travels through the West, and doubtlessly, to no small extent, by his encounters with Westerners.

With the biographical journey concluded, we now turn to the core teachings of Hazrat Inayat Khan. These teachings reflect an integration of his Eastern roots and Western experiences, exploring themes such as Purification, The Heart, Music, and God – the pillars of his unique approach to Sufism.

Notes

1 Hazrat Inayat Khan, *The Sufi Message: Volume 12, Confessions: Autobiographical Essays of Hazrat Inayat Khan: The Early Years* (Delhi: Motilal Banarsidass, 1988).
2 Elise Guillaume-Shamhart and Munira Van Voorst van Beest, eds., *The Biography of Pir-o-Murshid Inayat Khan* (London and The Hague: East-West Publications, 1979), 70.
3 Hazrat Inayat Khan, *The Sufi Message: Volume 12, Confessions: Autobiographical Essays of Hazrat Inayat Khan: The Early Years* (Delhi: Motilal Banarsidass, 1988).
4 Hazrat Inayat Khan, *The Unity of Religious Ideals: The Spiritual Hierarchy, Government, vol. 9 of The Sufi Message* (Delhi: Motilal Banarsidass, 1988).
5 Hazrat Inayat Khan, *In an Eastern Rose Garden: The Master Mind, vol. 7 of The Sufi Message* (Delhi: Motilal Banarsidass, 1988).
6 Elise Guillaume-Shamhart and Munira Van Voorst van Beest, eds., *The Biography of Pir-o-Murshid Inayat Khan* (London and The Hague: East-West Publications, 1979), 185.
7 Elise Guillaume-Shamhart and Munira Van Voorst van Beest, eds., *The Biography of Pir-o-Murshid Inayat Khan* (London and The Hague: East-West Publications, 1979), 183.
8 Elise Guillaume-Shamhart and Munira Van Voorst van Beest, eds., *The Biography of Pir-o-Murshid Inayat Khan* (London and The Hague: East-West Publications, 1979), 234–240.
9 Pir-o-Murshid Inayat Khan, *The Story of My Mystical Life*, reported by Dr. O.C. Gruner (Leeds, June 10, 1919), 5.
10 Saida van Tuyll van Serooskerken, *Memories of Murshid*, private collection, part of the Smith Kerbert Collection, archived at the Nekbakht Foundation, Suresnes, France.
11 Elise Guillaume-Shamhart and Munira Van Voorst van Beest, eds., *The Biography of Pir-o-Murshid Inayat Khan* (London and The Hague: East-West Publications, 1979), 168.
12 Hazrat Inayat Khan, *In an Eastern Rose Garden, Vol. 7 of The Sufi Message of Hazrat Inayat Khan* (Delhi: Motilal Banarsidass, 1989), 221–228; Hazrat Inayat Khan, *The Unity of Religious Ideals*, Vol. 9 of *The Sufi Message of Hazrat Inayat Khan* (Delhi: Motilal Banarsidass, 1990), 127, 141; Karin Jironet, *The Image of Spiritual Liberty in the Sufi Movement Following Hazrat Inayat Khan* (Leuven: Peeters Publishers, 2002), 130–134.
13 See, for example, Hofstede, 1994, on 'power distance' and 'individualism and collectivism' in *Cultures and Organizations: Intercultural Cooperation and Its Importance for Survival.*
14 Elise Guillaume-Shamhart and Munira Van Voorst van Beest, eds., *The Biography of Pir-o-Murshid Inayat Khan* (London and The Hague: East-West Publications, 1979), 179.
15 Kismet Dorothea Stam, *Diary*, 1923–1926.

Chapter 6

Self-Realization
The Path to the Divine

Consciousness

For Hazrat Inayat Khan, self-realization is the pinnacle of human attainment. It means the revealing of the soul's deepest knowledge. Self-realization is at once a journey and a destination, a process of awakening that refines perception, expands consciousness, and dissolves the barriers of separation. Unlike a linear path with fixed milestones, self-realization comes in waves and cycles, deepening with experience and insight. Having said that, consciousness also develops in stages. Sufi teachings describe five successive stages of awareness: *Nasut, Malakut, Jabarut, Lahut,* and *Hahut.* Together these stages suggest that human consciousness is not fixed but capable of vast expansion, leading from sensory awareness to union with the Divine.

In *A Sufi Message of Spiritual Liberty,* Inayat Khan affirms that self-realization means ultimately knowing oneself, gradually rising through the stages of manifestation until consciousness draws near to divine consciousness, even if only for a moment.

Inayat Khan speaks of different modalities of self-realization, each offering its own gateway to higher awareness and inner freedom. Among these, Purification, Heart, Music, and God emerge as central themes, interwoven throughout his teachings. They do not stand apart but move into and through each other, shaping transformation in both inner awakening and outer expression in life.

A Sufi Message of Spiritual Liberty serves as a starting point, not only because it was the only book Inayat Khan wrote himself in English, but because it offers a clear, living expression of his vision. From there, I draw on his collected works, *The Sufi Message,* to deepen the exploration.

Before we proceed, let us pause and read Inayat Khan's own words on self-realization:

The outcome of the whole of manifestation seems to be its knowledge; therefore, it is knowledge alone that can be called the purpose of the whole creation. It is not the knowledge of why and where that can be the purpose of life; it is the knowledge that gives complete satisfaction. There remains no part of one's

DOI: 10.4324/9781003431336-6

Figure 6.1 Hazrat Inayat Khan seated on the outdoor steps of Fazal Manzil, Suresnes 1923.

being that is hungry. There is a feeling of everlasting satisfaction in knowing something that the knower can never put into words. It is this knowledge that mystics call self-realization.[1]

For Hazrat Inayat Khan, self-realization is not about acquiring something new but about awakening to what is already present. It is a shift in perception that leads to liberation, dissolving the illusion of separation between the individual and the divine. This transformation requires a refinement of being, an attunement to the higher vibration of the soul. Knowing and intellectual understanding follow. But what does it take to reach this state?

Three principles mark the path: initiation, renunciation, and remembrance. Each carries its own practices and challenges. The path toward God is not one of knowledge alone but of lived experience, a journey that calls the seeker's whole being. In the Sufi tradition, this path is illuminated through *bayat*, the initiation that binds guide and disciple in trust. *Bayat* is a covenant. With this initiation, each seeker begins a journey that requires openness to receive guidance, to observe the individually prescribed practices, and to witness their effects on the inner life and in daily living. To walk this path requires sincerity, faithfulness, and an undoubting heart. Half-heartedness has no place here. One who hesitates at the threshold may sit there for a thousand years and never glimpse the goal, while one who surrenders and proceeds will, through contemplation and devotion, find the way revealing itself beneath their feet.

Throughout history, seekers have renounced family, wealth, and status, retreating into solitude in search of the divine. But Inayat Khan's Sufi path does not advocate withdrawal from life. Instead, it teaches that true renunciation is not about rejecting the world, but about seeing through it and no longer being bound by material goods and relationships. Praise and blame, pleasure and pain, success and failure all lose their hold when seen for what they are: passing waves on the ocean of existence.

Inayat Khan also emphasizes that prayers and spiritual practice alone are insufficient – the intention behind the practice determines its impact. If pursued for selfish purposes or worldly power, spiritual attainment becomes hollow. But when approached with humility and a genuine longing for truth, that attitude becomes the path.

He explains how this way the value of worldly things changes, much like the scenery on a stage ceases to be a palace once the illusion is recognized.

True renunciation requires courage. It is through such attitude or act of renunciation that the false ego's grip gradually dissolves along with worldly desires and egoistic ambition.

The divine may then be *remembered* as being enshrined within, which is a tremendous feeling. Inayat Khan at the same time warns that such "intoxication" diminishes the potential of the remembrance. To contiguously approach God with the innocence of a child, with gratitude and trust he says, may, as far as possible, safeguard against such exhilaration that may occur spontaneously in early training.

Seeing and Shifting through the Veils

When one engages in the spiritual practices prescribed with sincerity, cultivates detachment, and lives in remembrance, something profound begins to take place.

The vibration of one's being refines, perception clears, and what once felt solid and separate reveals itself as fluid and interconnected. Through this shift in perception, the restless search for happiness ends, for one realizes it was never missing.

Such a shift in understanding rests on *unlearning* the mind's persuasions and fixed ideas of material reality *and awakening to a life where knowledge and happiness are no longer sought but lived.*

Inayat Khan reminds us that the purpose of life is not the accumulation of knowledge but the direct experience of an inner knowing that brings unshakable fulfillment. It is the kind of knowing that leaves nothing unsatisfied but fills every part of one's being with joy and peace.

In the following, we turn to four central *practices* of this Sufi path - Purification, Heart, Music, and God- each, and together, a doorway into self-realization.

Purification

Purification is the cornerstone of the Sufi path, the alchemical process through which the disciple gradually approaches their essential nature beyond the illusions built up by the mind. It is an inner refinement, a gradual unveiling of the soul's radiance by stripping away the layers of ego, attachment, and desire.

Inayat Khan speaks of the "false ego" (*nafs*) that "feeds on weakness" and is reinforced by our complaints, preferences, and impulses. The false ego, when perceived as a barrier, is to be refined rather than crushed for it to become an ally of the soul. Once dedicated to such purification process, one begins to tame the *nafs* through spiritual practices, meaning learning how to turning the false ego's gaze inward.

Inayat Khan expresses this process with a simple yet profound analogy: To purify oneself is to restore one's being to its essential nature.

The Dimensions of Purification

Just as purification is not a single act, it is also not confined to a single aspect of life. It must touch every dimension of one's being. The journey begins with shedding the idea of "me" as an isolated entity with layers of thought, feeling, and ego that one so easily attaches to.

Mystics do not deny these layers but learn to see through them, so that space opens for divine presence. In this sense, purification is not an end but a beginning.

With this in mind, we can now follow how purification evolves through body, mind, heart, and soul.

Purification of the Body

The body, as the temple of the soul, is best be purified when its elements – earth, water, fire, air, and ether – are in balance. This harmony requires rhythm: movement and stillness, nourishment and restraint.

Inayat Khan emphasizes that purification of the body is a state where every vein and vessel is open and free, every movement and breath aligned with the rhythm of life.

Modern life, he warns, tends toward imbalance where activity overwhelms repose and disrupts that inner harmony which is needed for contemplation and spiritual realization to occur:

> The great error of this age is that activity has increased so much that there is little margin left for repose. Repose is the secret of contemplation and meditation, the secret of getting in tune with that aspect of life which is the essence of all things.[2]

Among the means of bodily purification, breath plays a fundamental role. In essence vibration, breath is central to both music and mysticism. Inayat Khan holds that mysticism has been founded on the science of breath as there is no mystic, whether Buddhist, Vedantic, or Sufi, who makes use of another process than that of breath. Breath is the first lesson and it is also the last. Breath, he holds, is the alpha and the omega.

Breath bridges body and soul aligning the *mureed* with the rhythm of creation. Inayat Khan teaches that through the rhythm of breath, the body regains balance, the mind becomes calm, and the soul's vitality restores.

Many different breathing practices are prescribed to *mureeds* but none compares to the elemental purification breathing practice. Performed at daybreak, before food, it is best practiced upright, preferably outdoors or by an open window. We return to this practice in more detail in Chapter 7.

After only a few days of conducting this practice, one begins to sense how the breath attunes different faculties, such as thought, speech and action, and how the mind grows silent and peaceful. One may also experience how through breath and repose, the body becomes a vessel for grace.

Purification of the Mind and Heart

The heart and the mind are not two separate faculties but two aspects of one and the same power of perception. Inayat Khan describes the mind as the surface of the heart, and the heart as the depth of the mind. Thus, mind and heart are not two things; they are the two aspects of one thing, the surface and the depth and when harmonized they reveal a single capacity of consciousness that perceives both the seen and the unseen.

The mind, with its faculties of thinking, reasoning, remembering, and identifying, shapes the lens through which we experience reality. But like a mirror clouded by dust, the mind gathers dust through impressions, judgments, and memories that obscure clarity. To hold onto these impressions is to halt life's natural movement. The *mureed* gradually learns to release these burdens so that perception becomes transparent again.

In support of this process the guide proposes a series of practices. Apart from prayer, often accompanied by gentle movements, the seeker may be instructed to repeat a *wazifa* received from the guide. A *wazifa* is one of the divine attributes — a name of God — whose repetition draws the heart nearer to its essence. For example, a *mureed* might be given the *wazifa ya-Hayy* ("the Living"), to be repeated with the breath: inhaling fully, then exhaling while softly reciting *ya-Hayy*. The number of repetitions may vary — thirty-three, ninety-nine — yet the essence lies less in counting than in the quality of intention. Through this remembrance, the heart gradually opens, becoming attuned to the divine qualities it invokes.

As the mind clears, the heart begins to stir. A power rises that removes inner obstacles, attracts what is needed, and brings the *mureed* in closer contact with the divine current. Inayat Khan speaks of the higher stream of love, a current that washes away the impurities of the heart just as water and breath cleanse the body. When allowed to be free, this love-stream makes the heart transparent. A purified heart yields purity in thought, feeling, and action.

At its deepest level, purification of the heart reveals what has always been present: happiness. Happiness is the natural state of the soul.

The soul is never impure, but it may be veiled. Its light may be obscured by what clings to it, for example, ego-identifications, fears, or ambitions. At times when the body is in a balanced state, the mind emptied, and the heart cleansed, the soul's own radiance begins to shine forth. The soul illuminates both inner and outer reality.

Purification at this level is not an act but a state of surrender. Breath dissolves into stillness. Time fades. What remains is presence. Thus, purification is not the erasure of the self but its gradual transformation. It is the remembering of the soul's original clarity.

Practices such as breath and forgiveness support this remembrance, but they do not *cause* it. They prepare the ground. The real work is the soul's own return to its rhythm, its own source.

Inayat Khan describes this subtle state in terms of *Hahut*, the plane of consciousness where the self is still, as pure being:

Sometimes, while you are sitting or standing with your eyes open, for one moment you do not see what is before your eyes, or someone speaks to you, and you have not heard . . . . A person feels: I am blank, but before he has time to say, 'I am blank' the state is gone. This is *Hahut*, the plane of consciousness where there is consciousness alone, without form and without name. This is the highest state, in which the consciousness is free from the self. This is liberation, towards which you are going, for which you are trying.[3]

Such is the mystic's awakening – moments when the soul merges with the divine and recognizes its eternal nature.

The Art of Emptying

There comes a time when we realize that what fills us is not always what nourishes us.

In the process of self-purification, even the rhythm of breath can reveal the subtle patterns of the mind. The shallowness or depth of one's breathing reflects the degree of openness within, showing how tension, fear, or longing imprint themselves upon the body. By attuning to the breath, one begins to restore harmony between the inner and outer currents of life — a return to balance that prepares the heart to awaken.

There is a moment in everyone's path when life itself whispers: Let it go. Not because we should reject life, but because we must make space – space to breathe, to listen, to perceive clearly.

Purification is not a rigid discipline, nor is it about striving for moral perfection. It is an art of emptying. It is a willingness, and at times an urge, to release what is not essential so that what *is* real can emerge.

It happens in many ways. Sometimes, we let go in sorrow. Other times, in relief. We may relinquish an old resentment, an ambition, a role we once played but have now outgrown. The act of surrender is rarely easy because it may feel like losing something. But what remains after purification is not loss, but essence.

Yet purification is not always what we might assume it to be. A river does not ask if its waters are clean before it washes away the past. The Ganges, thick with silt and human offering, is not pure by physical standards, yet it draws millions of pilgrims who enter its currents not to remove dirt but to be cleansed in a way that has nothing to do with the body. They come because the river is alive with meaning, charged with devotion, a vessel of transmission. The impurity pilgrims seek to remove is not on the skin but in the soul.

This is what Inayat Khan means when he says that purification is not just of the surface but of the veins. In many cultures, purity is often reduced to outward cleanliness, ritual correctness, or moral strictness. But for the mystic, true purification runs far deeper. It is not about what is removed but what is revealed.

The mystic does not purify for the sake of purity itself. As the dust settles, the mirror of the heart reflects more light. And with that light comes something simple, something powerful: clarity.

The Heart

The heart has long been revered in spiritual traditions as more than a physical organ. Inayat Khan sees the heart as the axis of being, a microcosm of the divine within human experience. For him, the heart is the meeting place of joy and sorrow, where the finite self encounters the infinite. It is here, in the depths of the heart, that the mysteries of existence manifest: love transforms into wisdom, pain becomes a gateway to clarity, and longing leads to union with the Beloved.

Here we explore the profound significance of the heart through its many dimensions: as the throne of God, the gateway to love, and the crucible of pain and joy. It invites the reader to discover the heart as the sacred ground where self-realization takes root, offering a path to seeing the divine in all things.

The Heart as the Throne of God?

Inayat Khan's teachings on the heart remind us that the heart is the key to understanding both the divine and ourselves. It is through the heart that we come to perceive the beauty of the world and also the light that shines within it. The mission on the spiritual journey of the heart is one of cleansing, awakening, and realignment with the soul's divine essence.

Inayat Khan explains,

> The heart of man is like a globe over the light of the soul. When the globe is dusty, naturally the light is dim; when it is cleaned, the light increases. In fact, the light is always the same; it is the fault of the globe when it is not clear.[4]

The heart, then, is not simply a symbol of divine connection: It is the throne itself, the seat of God within the human being, luminous and profound, and the meeting ground of the seen and unseen.

It is the gateway to feeling, a dedicated vessel poised between the material and the spiritual. As the soul's first emissary, the heart receives its subtle impressions and transmits them outward, shaping the contours of human experience.

The Aspects of the Heart

In Sufi mysticism the heart is the seat of divine intelligence and the instrument through which the ego (*nafs*) awakens to the presence of the soul (*ruh* in Persian). Unlike the intellect, which dissects and categorizes, the heart perceives through unity. It does not seek to know the divine as an object but to become transparent to its presence.

Sufi teachings describe the disclosing of the heart in four dimensions, each revealing a different aspect of its luminous intelligence. The first is *'Arsh,* the exaltation of divine will, where the heart links with a force greater than itself, surrendering to the infinite. This is the throne upon which divine intention is received, where the seeker learns to relinquish personal striving and move in harmony with the unseen currents of existence.

Next is *Kursi,* the seat of justice and discernment, where wisdom and clarity originate. Here, the heart refines its vision, distinguishing truth from illusion, right action from misstep. It is not a place of cold judgment but of profound balance, where decisions result from alliance with divine order rather than personal impulse. It is the light of truth that gives us the power to see into our difficulty as well as shows us the way out of it.

Beyond discernment lies *Lawh*, the wellspring of inspiration. Here the heart becomes a living tablet upon which divine impressions are inscribed. It is the space of revelation, where knowledge beyond intellect arrives unbidden, appearing as sudden insight, a whisper of intuition, or the inexplicable certainty that one is being led.

Then, there is *Kalam*, the fountain of intuition, where words spring from a source deeper than the self. At this stage, the heart becomes an instrument of divine expression, a mirror in which truth reveals itself without distortion.

Inayat Khan draws a distinction between consciousness and the soul, likening the latter to consciousness to its reflection. He explains,

The difference between consciousness and the soul is that the soul is like a mirror, and the consciousness is a mirror which shows a reflection in it.[5]

The Arabic concept of *ruh* and the Sanskrit *atman* both speak to this essence, namely the breath of the eternal, animating all life. The heart's journey is to polish itself so completely that it no longer holds an image of its own but becomes a perfect reflection of the divine.

Through these stages, the heart transforms from a chamber of personal longing into a gateway of infinite presence. No longer purely the center of emotion, it becomes the axis where Heaven and Earth meet – the place where the seeker comes to know the Self and the soul's eternal belonging.

The Radiance of Creation

Every atom of existence holds a spark of divine radiance, for all creation emanates from the heavenly source. Even the dust beneath our feet glimmers with an inner light, testifying to its celestial origin. Yet, our light is often veiled, buried beneath the illusions of ego and the restless projections of the mind.

When the heart awakens, this radiance transpires like a forgotten melody, revealing the luminous essence that has always been present. Inayat Khan teaches that the purification of the heart allows this light to shine outward, transforming not only the individual but also their surroundings.

"When this radiance shines out," he says, it shows itself not only through the countenance and expression of a man, but even in the man's atmosphere." The soul-power, so to speak, freely projects outward, and the surroundings feel it.[6]

The Alchemy of Love

In its journey toward manifestation, intelligence takes its next step as love. Love ignites the heart, transforming it into a transparent vessel through which the soul's intelligence can shine. Without this flame, intelligence remains in darkness, yearning for the light.

Love's transformative power lies in its ability to dissolve the false self and awaken the heart. The Sufi sees love not as a fleeting pleasure but as the divine force that clears the veils of separation. When love kindles the heart, it opens the door to self-realization, allowing the individual to recognize their unity with the divine.

Purification: The Path to Illumination

The purification of the heart is the foundation of the Sufi path. Through renunciation and surrender, the heart is cleansed, becoming a vessel for divine love. This inner refinement dissolves the layers of fear, bitterness, and ego that obscure the soul's light.

Through devotion, the heart becomes intoxicated with divine love. Inayat Khan describes *Kouthar,* the sacred wine, as "the intoxicating influence of spiritual ecstasy, which is hidden in the heart as love".[7] Such intoxication leads to the state of the *Sahib-e Dil,* the awakened heart or master-mind. Inayat Khan reminds us that when the heart awakens and remains awake, its magnetism grows ever stronger, attracting what words cannot describe; for the power of the heart is the power of God. When the heart is awake, it can hear the whisper that speaks within.

The Awakened Heart: A Mirror of the Beloved

When the heart awakens, it becomes a reflection of divine beauty. No longer fragmented by surface illusions, the awakened heart sees unity in all creation. Every face, every flower, every mountain becomes a reflection of the divine Beloved.

Mystics teach that the very purpose of creation lies in this recognition. The perfect Being, in infinite love, brought beauty into existence to behold itself. Thus, the Sufi greets life with the eternal refrain: " *'Ishq Allah, Ma'bud Allah"* – God is love, and God is the Beloved.

Self-Realization Through the Heart

Self-realization through the heart is the awakening to one's divine nature, the alignment of the individual self with the universal soul. It is the gradual unveiling of truth, peeling away the layers of distress and illusion that obscure the inner light.

Inayat Khan's emphasis on pain over pleasure offers a counterintuitive lens through which to understand this journey. Pain is not an obstacle but the refining fire that purifies the heart, breaking through to the essence of love and allowing the soul's radiance to emerge.

Through love – both as an experience of longing and as a transformative force – the heart becomes purified, transparent, and luminous, reflecting the light of the soul. Such awakening transforms perception, allowing one to see beyond appearances and recognize the divine presence in all things. The heart becomes the seat of wisdom, the source of compassion, and the gateway to union with the Beloved.

Sorrow and Joy: The Paradoxes of Life

Inayat Khan Inayat Khan's teachings remind us that pain is the heart's greatest gift. Unlike pleasure, which lulls the heart into complacency, pain awakens its depths.

The heart is not living until it has experienced pain, he writes, revealing the paradox that love's ache is what unites the lover with the Beloved.

Every wound inflicted by life becomes a portal through which the heart encounters the divine. Sorrow refines the heart, breaking through its hardness and allowing the radiance of the soul to emerge. Like a diamond formed under pressure or a seed split open in darkness, the heart's suffering reveals its hidden brilliance.

To turn away from this pain is to deny the heart its awakening, Inayat Khan warns. It is through sorrow that the heart gains the strength to reflect the light of the soul and the capacity to see the Beloved in all things.

Inayat Khan sees pain not as punishment, nor as opposed to joy. Rather, it is the fire that refines the heart, making it vast enough to contain love, wisdom, and beauty in their fullest form. The heart, like a vessel, can only hold what it has space for. Sorrow carves out that space. The more it is hollowed, the more deeply joy can pour in. Just as music needs both sound and silence, and just as a pearl forms only after an irritation wounds the shell, so too does the heart gain its depth through what it endures. But what does it mean for the heart to truly break? Inayat Khan teaches that the heart's breaking is not its undoing but its awakening. A heart that has never known sorrow has not yet discovered its full capacity for love. He likens the breaking of the heart to the cracking of a shell – the outer layer must be shattered for the life within to emerge. Just as a bud must break open to become a flower, so too must the heart open through pain to reveal its deeper truth. This is why he does not speak of suffering as something to avoid, nor does he encourage retreat into pleasure alone. Instead, he invites the seeker to experience life in its fullness, knowing that both light and shadow are part of the same divine tapestry. There are moments when the heart breaks – not only in grief but in awe, in longing, in unbearable beauty. And in those moments, something inside us opens. We glimpse, if only for an instant, that we are more than our small selves – that we belong to something greater, something eternal. This is why sorrow, when fully accepted, does not diminish us; it deepens us. The Sufi does not ask, "How can I avoid pain?" but rather, "How can I make my heart vast enough to hold it all?" And so, sorrow and joy are no longer opposites. They are lovers in the same embrace, drawing us ever closer to the heart's ultimate truth: love itself.

Music

Unveiling the Divine Through Sound and Silence

Across cultures and traditions, music has been revered as a language of the soul, capable of expressing what words cannot. For Inayat Khan, music was the sacred bridge to the divine, a means of awakening the heart and attuning the self to the eternal rhythm of existence. He saw music as the essence of life itself, carrying within it the mysteries of Love, Harmony, and Beauty; the pillars he designated to the spiritual path. Love is the nature of life, beauty is the outcome of life, harmony is the means by which life accomplishes its purpose. Love is the only power that has created, or that can create. It is those who have love of music who can give their music to the world.

Let us now explore the transformative power of music in a few of its aspects – its silent vibrations shaping the world around us, its capacity to elevate us into states of unity and ecstasy, and its subtle, celestial echoes that guide the soul toward the divine Beloved

The Inner Journey

For Inayat Khan, the journey toward divine attunement begins with learning to perceive the subtle language of life, a language expressed in the expressions, gestures, and movements of all living beings. While no fixed rule exists for deciphering this silent conversation, the seeker is guided by two essential faculties: keen observation of human nature and a finely developed intuition. These allow one to discern the hidden currents behind outward expressions. Yet, even those who master this understanding may find it difficult to translate it into words, for it belongs to a realm that exists beyond speech, a realm of pure resonance.

Inayat Khan likened this resonance to music itself as every action, word, and presence carry a unique vibration, revealing the soul behind it. To him, music was not merely sound but a living expression of the soul, much like poetry, where the true meaning lies not in the words themselves but in the music they hold between the lines.

The true listener feels the silence between the notes just as the perceptive soul sees beyond the surface of life to its hidden harmonies. This attunement to the unseen forms the very foundation of Inayat Khan's mystical journey, where understanding develops through vibrational awareness of what links all things in existence.

Music as the Royal Road to Harmony

For Inayat Khan, music was the royal road to harmony, a bridge to the divine. He experienced God as hidden in music, describing how deep listening opens a creative dialogue between the listener and the divine. This silent exchange shaped his own mystical expression, particularly in his early years in the West, where he often taught not through words, but through music itself. In these moments, he would invite a few *mureeds* into his room, play his instrument, and leave them to depart in silence, without words, questions, or applause. In the vibrations of the music, they were invited to find what language could not convey.

In his seminal work *The Mysticism of Sound*, Inayat Khan explores music as the precursor to speech, suggesting that music is hidden within words, just as the soul is hidden within the body. Ancient sacred messages, such as the *Song of Solomon* or the *Gathas of Zoroaster*, were sung rather than spoken, preserving the resonance of the divine. For Inayat Khan, this reflected a profound truth: music is the soul's native language, transcending intellect and speaking directly to the heart.

The Silent Music of Atmosphere

Inayat Khan also spoke of the silent music that permeates all things. Every soul, he observed, radiates an influence that fills the atmosphere, much like light or heat emanates its warmth. This influence is not bound by walls or distance – it lingers, shaping the space long after the person has left. Sensitive souls can perceive it in a room, in the imprint left on a chair, or even in an object like a rosary or a pen.

Unlike sound, which reaches the heart through the ears, this silent music touches the soul directly. For Inayat Khan, it was a testament to the interconnectedness of all existence, a reminder that everything carries the imprint of its source. In this way, he taught that the vibrations we leave behind shape the world as profoundly as the actions we take.

To enhance awareness of this inner dimension Inayat Khan also taught *Shagal*, an advanced practice known as the art of listening to the inner sound. In this practice, the senses, are gradually drawn inward, one by one, away from outer distraction, until one perceives the subtle current that underlies all existence — the "soundless sound". In *Shagal*, one listens not with the physical ear but with the heart's inner ear, a concentration that awakens awareness of vibration as the ground of being. Through this attunement, one realizes that music is not only something played or heard, but the very hum of life itself, always present when the senses withdraw from noise.

Music and the Soul's Ascent

Inayat Khan often described music as *ghiza'-i ruh*, "the food of the soul". For him, music was a sacred science, a means through which the soul could ascend to higher spiritual spheres. Just as a diamond cuts a diamond, so too could musical vibrations dissolve the denser layers of physical and mental existence, allowing one to move beyond the limitations of ordinary perception.

He identified five dimensions of musical experience, each corresponding to a stage in the soul's journey:

Music that induces movement (*tarab*) engages the body, awakening a rhythm that resonates with life itself.

Music that appeals to the intellect (*raga*) refines the mind, offering intricate structures that evoke deeper contemplation.

Music that stirs the heart (*qul*) unlocks the doors of feeling, opening pathways of longing and devotion.

Music that is heard in vision (*nida*) speaks to the seeker in dreams and inspiration, bridging the visible and invisible realms.

And finally, music in its most abstract form (*saut*) becomes a celestial vibration, a resonance beyond form, where sound itself dissolves into pure presence.

Through these 5 dimensions, music becomes a passageway harmonizing the *mureed* with both the material and spiritual worlds. It was no accident that Sufi mystics such as Jalal ad-Din Rumi and Khwaja Mu'in ad-Din Chishti wove music into their spiritual disciplines, using it as a means to elevate the soul toward eternal peace.

For Inayat Khan, the experience of sound was never separate from the experience of the divine; music was both the path and the arrival.

The Ecstasy of Union

Among the Sufis, the practice of *sama'*, the sacred art of listening, is a doorway to ecstasy, *wajd*, the rapture in which the boundaries of self dissolve and one is drawn into the Divine Presence. Inayat Khan spoke of this ecstasy as a blessed bath of love, a moment when the soul glimpses the Beloved as an overwhelming reality.

For the Sufis, *sama'* has always been more than an aesthetic or emotional experience – it is a form of meditation, a vehicle of transformation. When the heart is touched by divine rapture, its expression may take many forms: silent tears, deep sighs, spontaneous movement. Each is a response to the ineffable. A sigh may clear the path to the unseen world, while tears cleanse the burden of ages. In these moments of *wajd*, knowledge beyond words and intellect comes unbidden – truths that no book can contain, no teacher can bestow.

The sanctified dance of ecstasy, *raqs*, still performed by Sufi dervishes, finds its origin in such moments of divine absorption. It is said that Rumi, lost in contemplation of the Creator, became so enraptured by the vision of divine unity that his very body began to turn, tracing circles upon the Earth in reflection of the celestial dance. The movement of his hands, the motion of his robe – each became an echo of that sublime encounter. What began as spontaneous rapture became ritual, a remembrance of the moment when the soul recognized itself in the Beloved.

In daily life, this may appear as being moved to tears by a melody, or finding that dancing in the kitchen or singing in the car restores balance after a day or moments of tension.

For Inayat Khan, music was the path itself, leading toward the ultimate union. It is through sound that the heart awakens, through rhythm that the body remembers its pulse, and through harmony that the soul realigns itself with the One. At the highest stage, music itself dissolves, and only love remains: the silent, all-pervading music of the cosmos.

The Resonance of the Soul: Music as a Path to Self-Realization

For Inayat Khan, music was the direct path to self-realization. He taught that music, in its highest form, reflects the divine order, where every vibration resonates with Love, creating Harmony, and manifesting as Beauty.

In the experience of music, the one encounters these three principles simultaneously, awakening the heart to its innate connection with the divine. Love, expressed through the soul's longing for unity, finds its echo in the harmonies of music, while Beauty reveals itself in the patterns and symmetry of sound.

In this way, music becomes a mirror through which the seeker perceives their own divine nature. Through deep attunement to music, the soul is refined, the heart purified, and the Self revealed, realizing the nature of the journey toward self-realization. And even today in our contemporary world, when thousands gather at concerts or festivals and lose themselves in sound, rhythm and song, there arises a fleeting dissolution of boundaries – a glimpse of unity, an echo of that same self-realization.

The Hidden Music of Being

There are moments when two souls meet and instantly recognize each other, as if vibrating on the same pitch. A room, a landscape, even a book can carry music – some are harmonious, some are dissonant, and some fall flat, devoid of life. Writing, too, has music. There are words that sing, words that lift, words that create an inner silence filled with meaning.

Inayat Khan was born into music as a sublime art form, and especially as a way of perceiving life itself. Beyond the instruments and melodies and sounds of his childhood, he came to understand music as vibration, frequency, resonance – as the silent hum of existence, the pulse that moves through all things. To him, attunement to music was attunement to God.

Inayat Khan explained that attunement means alignment with the subtle music of being itself. When the soul is finely tuned, it can perceive the higher harmonies – the currents of truth beneath all things. This is why purification is essential. The body, the heart, and the mind must be cleansed in order to endure the frequencies of higher consciousness. A being that is heavy with discord cannot resonate with the divine.

Inayat Khan taught that every soul carries a unique note, a vibration that is its true self. To live in alignment with this note is to live in harmony with oneself, with others, and with the cosmos. When there is dissonance, it is felt, for instance, in the form of restlessness, disconnection, uncertainty. But when the soul returns to its note, it remembers: it belongs, it is held, it is part of the great symphony of existence.

God

Inayat Khan's teachings reveal God as the all-pervading existence in which all things live, move, and have their being. Though the essence of God remains beyond human comprehension, the divine can be approached through the heart, through love, and through mystical experience. To Inayat Khan, God is both transcendent – vast, unfathomable, beyond reach – and at the same time, immanent – closer than breath, woven into the very fabric of one's soul.

The Manifestation of God in Creation

The journey of manifestation begins with sound, the first vibration that awakens intelligence to existence. Light, or color, follows as the second aspect, illuminating creation. In sacred traditions across cultures, this truth is reflected. The Bible declares, "In the beginning was the Word, and the Word was God". Elsewhere, it states, "First was the Word, and then came Light". Light, inseparable from color, manifests as the very essence of illumination. In the Vedanta, this wisdom echoes in the understanding that the first aspect of the Creator – the Source from which all creation manifested – was sound. Similarly, in the Qur'an, the first divine command emerges as "Give us a sound," and through that utterance, creation begins.

Manifestation, by its nature, emanates through duality, and within this duality, God reveals himself in two distinct aspects. In one, He remains untouched, unbound, and beyond creation – pure consciousness, absolute and infinite. The mystics call this Allah, the Eternal beyond manifestation. In the other, He is the very fabric of existence itself, the essence of the visible and invisible worlds.

Creation, for God, is effortless – a mere breath, a whisper of reality. Yet, for human beings, it is an immense and mysterious journey, where divine unity appears refracted through the lens of separation. If God is called the Good, it is a name of profound beauty. But in the realm of duality, where opposites define experience, what begins as pure goodness may appear as its shadowed reflection. Light, passing through the prism of the earthly realm, takes on infinite forms, some radiant, some obscured, yet all belonging to the same source.

Each of us partakes in this manifestation of duality, embodying both the Good and its veiled counterpart. The latter, known in Sufi tradition as *nafs*, is the aspect of the ego that causes disharmony within oneself, with others, and with the divine. It appears as unruliness in thought, word, and action, obscuring the deeper truth that beyond duality, all is one.

The Four States of the Absolute

The Qur'an speaks of the origins of creation with the words: "The world was created out of darkness". This darkness is the Unknown – a state beyond the reach of human perception, imagination, or comprehension. It is the unmanifest, the silence before the first sound, the stillness before the first light.

The Unknown (Darkness)

In the beginning, existence was formless, boundless, and beyond all description. Sufi mystics speak of this as the One Only Being – absolute, omnipotent, omnipresent, and eternal. It is nameless and formless, birthless and deathless, yet it is the root of all existence. To those who have awakened, it is perfect rest, infinite peace, the unshaken stillness upon which the universe rests.

The Awakening of Consciousness

Out of this infinite stillness arose the first awakening of consciousness, a realization of existence itself. Like a flawless mirror reflecting nothing yet, it was pure and unlimited. In the Sufi tradition, this is known as *'Ilm* – a state of self-awareness yet without form, space, or movement. Inayat Khan defines *'Ilm* as the original state of consciousness, the pure intelligence.

The Movement Toward Manifestation

Pure Intelligence carried within it a hidden yearning. Just as eyes seek something to see and ears long for sound, intelligence, by its nature, longs to experience. This longing, the first motion toward creation, is called love. The Sufis name this force *'Ishq* – the primal love that set the cosmos into motion, drawing the unmanifest toward manifestation. Inayat Khan adds that intelligence and love are in essence the same, saying that as among animals intelligence begins to develop, so also does love begin to show itself.

Creation

From this Love, or Will, Intelligence began to extend outward, expanding from its formless state. Passing through countless veils of names and forms, it gradually descended into material existence. The Sufis call this plane *Insan*, the human experience of earthly life, where Intelligence perceives itself in an endless multiplicity of shapes and forms. This final state, in which the Intelligence has realized itself in form, is called *Wujud*, the reality of material existence, whose purpose it is to be loved. Inayat Khan emphasizes that love could not manifest unless there were an object to love. Love, he says, is the desire to be conscious of the object of love.

At this culmination, the human being stands at the threshold of realization. When humanity awakens to the knowledge of its original state, the timeless realm from which all arose, it fulfills its purpose. In this moment, the human being becomes the ideal of creation, conscious of that eternal state where Spirit first rested, unshaped by form, untouched by experience.

Yet, as each fragment of this manifestation descends into form, it forgets its origin, proclaiming, "I," unaware of the One from whom it emerged. But when the veil of separation is lifted, and the individual intelligence remembers its immortal nature, it becomes master of all states of being. This, Inayat Khan holds, is the ideal being whose bliss transcends the limitations of Earth and cannot be surpassed even in Heaven.

Shuhud: The Witnessing of Truth

At the highest stage of realization, the knower becomes known to himself. This state is called *Shuhud*, the witnessing of eternal truth. Here, the aim of life finds its fulfillment, for in *Shuhud*, the seeker becomes the sought, and the witness becomes the witnessed.

Consciousness of *Shuhud* can be attained by closing the eyes to the limited self and opening the heart to God. Not that distant God or king pictured in the heavens, but the God of all perfection, at once immanent and transcendent. He is in Heaven and on Earth, within and without. He is visible, tangible, audible, and perceptible, yet forever beyond comprehension. No eyes have seen Him, no hands have touched Him, yet He remains the eternal presence, the witness of all creation.

The Universal Presence

The oneness of God is at the heart of Sufi understanding. From this fundamental truth emerge two profound interpretations: *Tawhid*, the affirmation of God's absolute unity, and *Wahdat al-Wujud*, the recognition of the unity of all existence. Though they may appear similar, they illuminate two distinct dimensions of divine reality.

Tawhid affirms the singularity of God in His absolute transcendence, maintaining a clear distinction between the Divine and creation. This perspective, embraced across all Islamic traditions, was emphasized by Ibn Taymiyyah (1263–1328), the influential Islamic scholar, theologian, and jurist. In his teachings, he underscored God's sovereignty and separateness, declaring Allah as the sole Creator, Sustainer, and Ruler of the universe.

Wahdat al-Wujud, an expression of *Tawhid*, reveals another dimension of divine unity – the immanence of God within creation. It is an invitation to experience the Divine directly, not as an article of faith but through spiritual practice, inner illumination, and mystical states of consciousness. Here, the boundary between the seeker and the sought dissolves, and the soul comes to recognize itself as a wave in the vast ocean of Divine Being.

Thus, *Tawhid* provides the theological foundation, while *Wahdat al-Wujud* offers the experiential depth – together forming a fuller vision of divine unity, encompassing both God's transcendence and immanence.

It is this felt experience of divine love and unity that illuminates the poetry of Jalal ad-Din Rumi (1207–1273), the great Persian poet, Sufi mystic, jurist, and theologian. In his verses, the lover and the Beloved are one, and the entire cosmos sings of the soul's longing for reunion. Through Rumi's words, the truth of *Wahdat al-Wujud* is not only understood but felt – as love, as longing, as the sacred rhythm of existence itself.

Love, Harmony, and Beauty

At the heart of Inayat Khan's teachings lies the divine triad of Love, Harmony, and Beauty – the essence of the One Being. Though this eternal truth is often obscured by the veil of multiplicity, it is reflected in every aspect of creation. Love binds all existence as one; Harmony reveals the balance and interconnectedness within that unity; and Beauty is the shining evidence of the divine presence, drawing the soul toward its source.

The human journey is a quest to rediscover this triad. As the heart awakens to love, the soul attunes to harmony, and the inner eye perceives beauty as a reflection of the Divine. In this awakening, the veils of separation and discord dissolve, and the seeker realizes that the purpose of life is not only to recognize these principles but to embody them – to live in love, to create harmony, and to find beauty in all things. Through this realization, the immanence of God becomes a living reality, present in every moment of existence.

As the heart opens and the inner eye begins to see, the veil of duality lifts, and the seeker discerns the presence of the Divine in all aspects of creation. There are countless beings in existence, yet there is ultimately only One – the Only Being. The rivers and mountains, too, are alive, revealing to the naked eye the oneness of all existence, the immanence of God. In awakening to this essence, outer distinctions fade and what remains is the eternal truth: the Divine is present in all things.

Though religions may appear diverse in their forms, their purpose is one: to cultivate and prepare the human heart for divine love. The Spirit of Guidance has, at different times, directed humanity to recognize the beauty of God reflected in the heavens, the trees, the mountains, and the flowing streams. At other times, it has unveiled the presence of the Divine in the animals and birds, declaring them holy.

As human consciousness evolved, so too did its perception of the Divine. It came to see that no being in creation surpasses man himself, for within man the divine light is most clearly manifest. With this realization, the worship of nature gave way to the recognition of God within the human heart, especially in those who have attained God-consciousness. Thus, step by step, humanity has been guided toward truth, toward the vision of the Divine within all things.

> There are sages who are moved to tears just by saying to themselves one word of essential truth, of abstract truth. What could have this effect? Is there some pain concealed in it? Is anything said to evoke sympathy? No, it is their ideal that is so high that they see the ideal beauty in the truth. The truth of being has become beautiful to them. Their beloved has become God, and when a word of truth is spoken in their hearing they are moved to tears. To these sages everything is a real manifestation of the beauty of God. If they hear music, in that music they feel God, in that music they see God. If they are standing before a picture, in the beauty of that picture they see their Beloved. If they are standing in a crowd, with all manner of faces, to them the whole picture is one harmony, one vision of the sublime, and they can see the whole beauty there. Whether it be desert, or sea, or sky, or land, whatever it is that is before their eyes has a vision of beauty to offer to them. And it is in this way that the whole of manifestation has become for them an immanence of the beauty of God.[8]

The Path to God

The soul is vast beyond measure, yet the way that leads from body to soul, from self to the Divine, is narrow. Straight is the gate, and narrow is the way, Inayat Khan reminds us, for any step taken in distraction leads the traveler astray. The path demands balance, neither excess nor deficiency, but a steady alignment with truth. To attain God-consciousness, one must make God a reality – a presence so deeply known that it ceases to be belief and becomes truth itself. In this state, the distinction between worshipper and worshipped dissolves; the seeker becomes what they seek.

Yet above all, the path to God is a path of love. Love is the complete merging of consciousness. The lover dissolves into the Beloved until no separation remains. It is love that refines the soul, awakening humility, patience, contentment, and kindness. It is love that grants the seeker courage, faithfulness, and gentleness, aligning them with the rhythm of the Absolute. And it is love that opens the final gateway, where the seeker steps beyond even the conception of self and God, dissolving into the boundless ocean of eternal bliss.

For Inayat Khan, the culmination of the journey is this union, where the soul no longer strives, no longer longs, no longer even names the Beloved. There is only oneness, beyond speech, beyond thought, beyond the need to return.

God, Freedom, and Freedom from the Self

In the Sufi path, self-realization is the process toward the soul's liberation from the confines of ego, desire, and worldly attachment. This liberation is a return rather than an escape from these worldly confines. True freedom lies in the willing and loving surrender to the Divine, where all false notions of self-assertion and separation dissolve. Such surrender is an act of profound trust and a courageous letting go that allows the soul to awaken to its infinite nature.

The Sufis call this surrender *fana'* the annihilation of the *nafs*, the self that clings to illusion and limitation. To the uninitiated, such a loss may seem like emptiness, an erasure of identity. Yet in truth, *fana'* is not obliteration but transformation. The one who surrenders does not vanish into nothingness but is lifted beyond selfhood into *baqa'*, the Eternal Life – where the soul no longer exists as a separate entity but as a vessel of divine expression.

This surrender is not a lofty state but rather a path sustained by practice. Inayat Khan teaches that the most central of these at this stage is the *zikr*, the remembrance of God. Through repeated invocation of *la illaha illa `Llah Hu* – there is no God but God-one gradually attunes to the being of God. The practice unites posture, breath, sound, and movement with the focus of mind and the quality of the heart. After the *zikr,* silence descends — an exquisite sense of being alive in body, mind, heart, and soul at once, present to life as vibration, as bliss.

After the zikr, silence descends — an exquisite sense of being alive in body, mind, heart, and soul at once, present to life as vibration, as bliss.

In the state of *fana'*, freedom is no longer defined by personal will but by alignment with the boundless presence of God. The liberated soul is free, not in the sense of acting without constraint, but in the sense of being without hindrance. No longer burdened by the weight of self, it moves effortlessly in harmony with the Divine – like a river returning to the ocean.

Here, self-realization is complete as the unbroken experience of truth. To be free of the self, *nafs*, is to be filled with God as a being found, resting in the vast, infinite presence of the Eternal. To live in this state is to embody the attributes of God, Love, Harmony and Beauty – as the natural fragrance of a liberated Soul.

A Living Presence, a Participatory Creation

God is not an idea. Not a doctrine, nor a distant presence to be reached only through prayers and rituals. God is the very pulse of existence – the breath within breath, the silence beneath sound, the unseen thread that holds all things together. To say "God" is not to name a being apart from creation but to name the One in whom creation is unveiled, moment by moment.

Inayat Khan did not teach of a God simply to be believed in; instead, he taught of a God to be experienced. A God who is not confined to scripture but is written in the fabric of the cosmos itself: in the rising of the sun, in the turning of the seasons, in the rhythm of the tides, in the stillness before an answer comes within, in the sudden knowing that you are not alone.

For Inayat Khan, to find God was not to remove oneself from life but to enter it fully, to participate in creation as an instrument through which God's presence radiates – to know that in every encounter with another person, with beauty, with sorrow, God is there, waiting to be recognized.

Yet, for most, this recognition does not come easily. The mind divides, names, and measures. It sees a world of separate things and asks, "Where is God?" It clings to certainty and misses the living mystery. But the heart – the heart knows. The heart feels the presence before the mind can explain it.

This is why the mystic turns inward, not to escape life, but to see it more clearly. The more the heart is purified, the more it can recognize God everywhere – in the face of a stranger, in the fragrance of a rose, in the way light moves across water, and most profoundly, in the silence that speaks when all else falls away.

God is not found elsewhere, not beyond the sky, nor in some distant heaven. God is here. Now. Closer than breath. Nearer than thought. The One in whom you live, move, and have your being.

Notes

1 Hazrat Inayat Khan, *The Sufi Message of Hazrat Inayat Khan: Volume 5. Metaphysics: The Experience of the Soul in Different Planes of Existence, Self-realization* (Delhi: Motilal Banarsidass, 1989), 250.
2 Hazrat Inayat Khan, *The Sufi Message: Volume 2, The Mysticism of Sound and Music* (Delhi: Motilal Banarsidass, 1988).
3 Hazrat Inayat Khan, *The Supplementary Papers: Mysticism 2, About the Five Planes.* Unpublished papers.
4 Hazrat Inayat Khan, *The Sufi Message of Hazrat Inayat Khan: Volume 5. Metaphysics: The Experience of the Soul Through the Different Planes of Existence, 3. The Destiny of the Soul, The Radiance of the Soul (2)* (Delhi: Motilal Banarsidass, 1989).

5 Hazrat Inayat Khan, *The Sufi Message: Volume 1, The Soul, Whence and Whither?* (Delhi: Motilal Banarsidass, 1988).
6 Hazrat Inayat Khan, *The Healing Papers: 2,2: The Spirit in the Flesh* (Delhi: Motilal Banarsidass, 1989).
7 Hazrat Inayat Khan, *The Sufi Message of Hazrat Inayat Khan: Volume 5, Aqibat: Life After Death*, 3. Heaven and Hell (Delhi: Motilal Banarsidass, 1989).
8 Hazrat Inayat Khan, *The Sufi Message: Volume 7, In an Eastern Rose Garden: Love, Harmony, and Beauty* (Delhi: Motilal Banarsidass, 1988).

Chapter 7

An Envisioned Dialogue

Where the Two Seas Meet

In this chapter, the boundaries of reality, time, and space are deliberately set aside. Here, imagination becomes the bridge that brings together the voices of Carl Jung and Hazrat Inayat Khan in a dialogue that never took place in historical fact but evolves vividly within the realm of possibility and meaning.

This is an imagined encounter, born from deep engagement with the works and legacies of these towering figures. While the dialogue presented is fictional, it is grounded in the timeless themes, insights, and questions that, as we have seen, emerge from their respective teachings.[1] In this space, Jung's analytical psychology meets Inayat Khan's mysticism, not merely to exchange ideas but to engage in a reflective interplay that transcends historical and cultural boundaries, inviting the reader to explore their own interior worlds.

The purpose of this chapter is not to assert truths but to evoke curiosity, self-reflection, and dialogue within the reader. By dissolving the constraints of the time-space continuum, the conversation becomes timeless, relevant as much to the past as to the present and future. It allows the reader to journey alongside Jung and Inayat Khan, experiencing their exchange as if seated in the same room, drawn into the enduring depths of their thought and spirit.

Readers are invited to suspend disbelief and join this imagined dialogue as participants, not simply as observers. The questions raised and themes explored – whether they pertain to the psyche, the soul, or the human condition – are meant to resonate personally and inspire further inquiry. Ultimately, this dialogue serves as an offering, a means to spark contemplation and perhaps even to uncover new facets of one's own lived experience.

The Liaison

The liaison that brings Carl Jung and Inayat Khan together for this invented dialogue is Lou Andreas-Salomé (1861–1937). She was born in St. Petersburg, Russia, to an intellectually stimulating environment, fostering her lifelong curiosity for religion, philosophy, and literature. At 19, she moved to Zurich, Switzerland, one of the few places in Europe at the time where women could study at a university level, and embarked on studies in theology, philosophy, and metaphysics at

DOI: 10.4324/9781003431336-7

the University of Zurich. At the age of 21, she moved to Rome, Italy, where she became part of a vibrant intellectual circle.

Lou was one of the first female psychoanalysts, a writer, and an intellectual who produced a rich body of work spanning fiction, philosophy, and psychoanalytic theory. She engaged deeply with existential and religious themes, reflected in works like *Jesus the Jew* (1894).

Lou's life was marked by her profound and often unconventional relationships with leading intellectuals of her time. She was a symbol of intellectual independence and a pioneer for women in philosophy and psychoanalysis. Her intellectual rigor and creativity left a lasting impression on thinkers such as Nietzsche, Freud, and Rilke.

How It All Came About

Lou, who was introduced to Inayat Khan by her friend Princess Sirtolov Lavrosky, was deeply impressed with his talk, in which Inayat Khan had expounded the ideal of Indian music with musical illustrations at the Imperial Conservatory of Music, Saint Petersburg, Russia, in early 1912. They had found a most rewarding moment to converse toward the end of the gathering, and it was therefore with great delight that they, only a few days later, found themselves at the same dinner party, which lasted well into the morning. As they said their hearty goodbyes, Lou knew intuitively that she wanted more of this atmosphere. Inayat Khan thought to himself that the warmth of the guests and Chaliapin's singing had touched him deeply because it reminded him of India.

Less than a year earlier Lou had sensed a similar enthusiasm during a conversation with Carl Jung at the 3rd Congress of Psychoanalysis in Weimar. She felt intensely how their shared connection around the unconscious as creativity deepened further than in such talks with her colleague Sigmund Freud, despite their romantic involvement. Jung observed that he was equally amazed and intrigued.

> That the only woman invited would approach me and without slightest hesitation start about how sexuality informs creativity! Naturally, I had to steer the ship and protect the young woman, so I simply brought her my ideas on the libido. She liked them very much,

Jung reflected when back at the hotel.

Lou stayed wide awake, went for a brisk walk, and searched her remembrances. Inayat Khan's music and the play he wrote when in St. Petersburg, *Shiva*, in collaboration with Serge Tolstoy, along with his expressed admiration for the Russian Dance . . . Jung's appetite for the unconscious, libido, archetypal images . . . this interplay evoked a timeless realization in Lou's mind. These ideas converged with her own deep-seated longing to revisit her Roman adventure: the academic commune she had envisioned as a young woman with Paul Ree and Friedrich Nietzsche in the early 1880s.

She knew then that the idea of the academic commune was not dead but very much alive. It just needed a new form: an intellectual soirée with dance and music performance! Art and science, she believed, would lead the way for humanity to a higher plane of consciousness.

When she learned that both Jung and Inayat Khan would be traveling – Jung returning from Africa along the Nile and Inayat Khan sailing from Venice to Port Said – the synchronicity struck her. Their itineraries would bring them both to Egypt at the same time. Inspired, Lou booked the Eastern Exchange Hotel, a cosmopolitan meeting place on the Mediterranean coast, and extended invitations to both men to join her there. Within a week, she received enthusiastic telegrams. Encouraged by their acceptance, she arranged the soirée, composed an invitation, and circulated it to intellectuals such as Leo Tolstoy, Serge Tolstoy, Mata Hari, Nietzsche, and, hesitantly, Rainer Maria Rilke, encouraging Jung and Inayat Khan to do the same.

On the night of the event, the room was full, with some guests standing along the back wall. A few additional chairs were brought in and carefully fitted into the space. She stood, and as she warm-heartedly welcomed everyone, she said,

It is with great pleasure that I welcome our esteemed guests: the Sufi Master Hazrat Inayat Khan and the Psychoanalyst Carl Jung. Welcome to this evening's gathering, where thought and imagination intersect to examine the timeless complexities of human consciousness.

Tonight, we are not just observers of ideas but participants in a dialogue that challenges us to consider the interplay between the conscious and unconscious. These two dimensions are not opposites but integral components of the human experience, each shaping and being shaped by the other across generations and cultures.

Love, in this context, is not simply an emotion but a dynamic process – a creative force that compels us to engage with the boundaries of our existence and to seek meaning beyond them. It is through these encounters that we find not fixed identities, but evolving perspectives that reflect both ourselves and the broader human condition.

Imagination, likewise, is not a trivial pursuit but an essential faculty of the mind, enabling us to impose order on chaos and to construct meaning where none is immediately apparent. This is alchemy transforming memory, intuition, and desire into something that transcends the self and resonates across time.

As we begin this dialogue, let us remain open to the exploration of these universal themes. This is an opportunity to engage with the profound questions that unite art, science, and philosophy in the pursuit of knowledge and self-awareness.

Let us begin.

Jung tapped the top of his pipe thoughtfully, lowering it to rest in his palm as he shifted slightly toward Inayat Khan. The Sufi master, calm and composed, gazed steadily into the hall, his eyes moving as though they were seeing beyond the faces before him – perceiving, perhaps, the souls beneath.

Breaking the momentary silence, Jung drew a deep breath. "You mentioned alchemy," he began, his voice measured but tinged with intensity. "It is a subject of profound interest to me. In fact, I believe it holds the key to the mystery of life."

Inayat Khan replied, completing his gaze into the audience,

Egypt, here, where the two seas meet, and now you and me, he nodded appreciatively towards Jung, is the land of the source of all wisdom. As we know, Abraham first brought the knowledge of mysticism from Egypt, where he was initiated into the most ancient order of esotericism. Upon his return, he chose Mecca as a sacred center – a place that must serve as the world's spiritual heart. Not only during the age of Islam did people make pilgrimage there, but even in earlier times, the pious revered Mecca as a sacred site.

Sufism, my line of initiation, meaning quietism, also traces its roots to Egypt. Its essence lies in the realm of quietism – a silence that holds the wisdom of the ages. But I look forward to our exchange, and to exploring these ideas together.

Jung tilted his head slightly, his brow furrowed. "Quietism . . .?"
"Yes," Inayat Khan said gently, his tone reflective.

The teachers – our way – is to awaken consciousness in the pupil, to illuminate what has become obscure or confined. Sometimes their method is so gentle, so nuanced, that the pupil does not even realize it is happening.

They do not say, 'You must not drink,' or, 'You must not gamble.' They never impose. Instead, the teacher employs the most wonderful way – to teach without words, to correct without speaking. What the teacher wishes to convey, he conveys silently, for when a truth is reduced to words, it is lost.

Jung nodded, leaning forward slightly.

For a long time, I struggled to understand Islam. I couldn't connect to it. But in Sudan, I had a meaningful experience. I was traveling down the Nile on a paddlewheel steamboat, and tied alongside it was a smaller boat. On it lay a thickset man – a Muslim. At night, I heard him calling out, '*Allah!*' It was like a pleading cry to the universe, infinite and raw. And then I understood – this is it!

His voice, stretching far into the endless expanse, seemed to hold the entire Arabic soul. It was deeply moving – a profound relationship to God, an Islamic Eros. I heard the same cry later in Delhi, at the great mosque. It was a longing that resonated from the very depths of the heart.

"There you have it!" Inayat Khan exclaimed, "It is the continuous awakening of the heart. Sufis of all ages, mystics of India, Persia, and Egypt, have held the awakening of the heart as the principal aim of life."

When the heart opens, virtue becomes natural. No one needs to teach it – it comes from within. True virtue cannot be imposed or learned like a habit; it must come effortlessly, like breath. Spirituality, you see, is natural. And if animals and birds can feel spiritual exaltation, why not we?

Jung's voice softened. "That was precisely my sense. *'Allah'* does not express fulfillment – it is a cry in the desert, under the endless sky. A call to a Being, omnipresent – like the wind. Formless, yet tangible, a feeling experience."

In my own work, I have found that *Khidr* – the guide associated with water, who initiated Moses – represents a symbolization or incarnation of this omnipresence.

Khidr, "The Green One!" Inayat Khan said, his enthusiasm quickening. "All Sufis, all mystics, belong to the lineage of *Khidr*! He appears to initiates at critical moments in their journey, always present in true initiation. At times, he has manifested as Elijah."
Jung's eyes opened wide,

Fascinating! I must tell you – one of my earliest initiations was, in fact, a profound disappointment. My Confirmation. I was filled with hope that now the secret of Christ would be revealed to me. But instead, I felt only a cold, heavy gloom.
    That experience transformed me, reshaping my understanding of Christ and Christianity. But what I really wish to share is a later initiation: my break with Freud . . .

Jung continued, his tone reflective, yet somewhat strained,

It was an overpowering disillusionment, one that threw me into psychological disorientation. In the midst of this chaos, I commenced dialogues with archetypes. And do you know who I first encountered during that time? Elijah! It is synchronicity that you mentioned him. It suggests that, in some deep roots, you and I are connected.

Elijah initiated me into the depths of my unconscious – not only my own, but the invisible world of all that is and ever was.

Inayat Khan nodded gravely. "A true encounter with omnipresence . . . Transformation . . . Transmutation."
Jung's voice deepened, carrying a note of reverence.

I would call it rebirth. Speaking of alchemy, here is a quote for you: 'The seeker after truth hears both the Stone and the Philosopher speaking as out of one mouth.' The Philosopher is, of course, Hermes, and the Stone – the Philosopher's Stone – is identical with Mercurius, Hermes himself, the guide and confidant of the alchemists who led them toward their goal.

Inayat Khan smiled,

The Green One – is he not continuously flowing forth as rebirth? In alchemy, Green is the base material to be boiled in the 'vas,' as you call it. Yet here, the base is also the center, as it transforms into the colors of rebirth. First comes the death of one form, *nigredo,* and from black to albedo, white – the differentiation of spirit and body. Then follows *citrinitas*, the yellowing, the Solar Light, and finally *rubedo,* the red – the stage of completion and wholeness.

"Exactly!" Jung interjected, "these symbols are profound reflections of psychological processes leading to the soul. The alchemists understood that it was not simply a matter of stirring in a cauldron under favorable stars. The real transformation happens within."

Inayat Khan inclined his head thoughtfully. "As I see it, these symbols may represent universal spiritual truths and are not only psychological constructs."

Lou Andreas-Salomé, who sensed some tension, intervened,

Hazrat Inayat Khan, I've heard it said that the Sufi path unfolds in distinct stages of consciousness. I'm intrigued – can you describe these stages for us? How do they guide one toward greater understanding?

Inayat Khan,

Ah, Lou, what a thoughtful question. Indeed, the journey of consciousness expands in stages, each one a step closer to the essence of the divine. Let us begin with the first stage, which we call *nasut*. This is the plane of the senses, the consciousness through which we experience the material world. When you see a rose, hear the wind, or taste something sweet, it is *nasut* at work. It is the consciousness of this body, grounded in what we can see, hear, touch, smell, and taste.

Lou, her eyes bright with curiosity, "And yet, that seems so . . . familiar, so fundamental. Is there a moment when one's awareness begins to transcend the senses?"

Hazrat Inayat Khan, nodding gently, as though affirming an unspoken truth,

Yes, exactly! The second stage is called *malakut*, the plane of thought and imagination, his voice quieter now, as though inviting his listeners into this next realm, it is where our consciousness begins to rise above the senses. Let me give you an example. Imagine a person walking past you, deeply immersed in thought. Their eyes are open, but they do not see you. Their ears are open, but they do not hear you. At that moment, their consciousness is not in *nasut* but in *malakut*. It is working through the mind, the imagination . . . beyond the body.

Lou, her voice soft, almost a whisper, "That sounds like a gateway to something even deeper."

Hazrat Inayat Khan, smiling faintly,

Indeed, it is. The third stage is *jabarut* – the consciousness of pure being. Imagine the peace of deep, dreamless sleep, where the mind is silent and the body at rest. *jabarut* is like this . . . but with the eyes wide open, fully awake. It is the life within us, the peace and purity that are always present, though often hidden.

He pauses, as though to let the idea settle, his hands resting lightly in his lap.

Many taste this peace in sleep, but for the mystic, *jabarut* is a waking reality – a blessing found through spiritual development.

Lou, nodding slowly while throwing a quick glance on the audience to check if they are following this which she recognizes, but do they? "And then? Is there yet another step?," she returns to Inayat Khan.

Hazrat Inayat Khan, his voice almost reverent now, not fond of speaking about the indescribable,

Yes, the next stage is *lahut*. Here, the consciousness rises from the material to the immaterial plane. It is a state of deeper peace, greater joy, and nearness to what we call . . . the divine essence. At this stage, one feels truly . . . free. Free of the limitations of the physical world, and yet profoundly connected to it.

Lou, after a long silence, her words coming softly,

And the final stage . . .?

Hazrat Inayat Khan, his countenance serene now and his voice carrying the weight of profound experience,

Hahut. This is the stage of merging with God. It is what some call Samadhi, the state where one dives into one's deepest self, where God is within. In *hahut*, one reaches the home of all intelligence, life, peace, and joy . . . a place where worry, fear, disease, and even death cannot enter.

He paused, his gaze lifting slightly, as if looking beyond the present moment into that experience. 'It is not a place of escape but of ultimate presence. The mystic in *hahut* knows that the deepest self and the divine are not separate . . . but one.'

The room was still, sharing in his experience.

After a substantial pause, Jung clasped his hands in his lap, his thoughts turning back to *Khidr*, Elijah, those archetypal figures that had guided his own inner journey. The connection stirred within him a realization – a deep truth he had often contemplated. His tone was eager yet measured, as if speaking to both himself and the gathering.

'The Cave', the title of the 18th Sura of the Koran, he began, pausing momentarily to choose his words, 'is a powerful symbol. Everyone has a cave within – a darkness behind consciousness. To enter it is to confront the unknown, the depths from which all libido, all psychic energy, stems. This descent into the unconscious starts a process of transformation, though at first, it happens without our awareness'. Jung's voice grew quieter as though he were touching upon a sacred mystery. 'It is all about rebirth – the transformation of what is mortal into what is immortal. In my view, this is where alchemy offers its greatest wisdom. This *is* the key to the mystery of life, showing us how the base material of our psyche can be transmuted into something eternal'.

Inayat Khan's voice softened. "In Sufi terminology, we call this *fana*' – freedom from the self, the limited self."
"All of them?" Jung asked, chuckling.
"Yes," Inayat Khan replied gently. "Ultimately, all of them. 'Die before death,' as we say."
Jung paused for a moment and then continued pensively. "And what remains?"
"Peace," Inayat Khan answered simply.
Jung's voice dropped, filled with awe.

And awe. Let me share something else. During a hospital stay, I suffered a heart attack. I experienced something remarkable – a vision of the earth from far away, luminous and blue. Everything I had wished for, thought of, or aimed at fell away. Yet something essential remained.

It was as if I carried within me all that I had ever experienced. It was me, and I was it – a fullness, a bliss within annihilation. Is that the peace you speak of?

Inayat Khan nodded, his expression serene. "Yes. I could not have said it better myself."
Jung:

This is then individuation and self-realization in the natural way, which often comes through dreams, but sometimes also through bodily, out-of-body experiences, such as . . . a heart attack. But let's say one consciously sets out to seek such an experience as a methodology – would it culminate in the same intensity of feeling?

Inayat Khan contemplated,

For some, for those with an open heart, yes. But everyone can progress far along the way simply by paying attention to the breath and practicing conscious breathing. We have a particular breathing practice that is very natural because it integrates the five elements and, in this way, aligns with alchemy.

Would you like me to show you? Perhaps it all comes back to you!

Lou raised her hand smilingly. "Perhaps those in the audience who wish to participate may join as well?"
Inayat Khan and Jung replied in unison, "Naturally."
Inayat Khan began, his tone steady and inviting.

Mysticism has always been founded on the science of breath. Breath, in essence, is vibration. It is the channel through which the innermost life expresses itself. Breath creates attunement between body and soul, encompassing balance, grounding, and alignment with the elements. Before we begin, please make yourselves comfortable, preferably seated with a straight back, feeling grounded and balanced. This posture itself creates balance. Let us now pause in silence for a moment before we engage in this practice.

He paused briefly, calmly scanning the audience. "We will breathe in rhythm with the elements, visualizing their colors to attune ourselves. Follow my guidance."
He raised his hand slightly, leading the group:

First, Earth Breath: Inhale through the nose and exhale through the nose. Visualize the color gold at the tip of your nose. Do this five times.

He waited for all in the group to complete before continuing.

Now, Water Breath: Inhale through the nose and exhale through the mouth. Visualize the color green at the bridge of your nose. Again, five breaths.

The rhythm of the group seemed to settle into harmony. Inayat Khan continued:

Next, Fire Breath: Inhale through the mouth and exhale through the nose. Visualize the color red at the third eye. Let this purify and energize your spirit.

As the exercise progressed, a sense of calm filled the room.

Now, Air Breath: Inhale through the mouth and exhale through the mouth, visualizing the color blue at the crown of your head. Feel the spaciousness it brings.

Finally, his voice softened.

Lastly, Ether Breath: Inhale and exhale through the nose, very gently, visualizing silvery transparency about 50 centimeters above your head. Let it rise and expand, connecting you to the infinite. Five times.

No one in the audience moved until, laboriously, Nietzsche, visibly touched by the exercise, stood and fished out a small, well-thumbed grey notebook and opened the pages. "Hrm, thank you. I appreciate this occasion and experience it as a genuine one. I wrote a small reflection. May I?" Lou made the ever-slightest nod.

Hrm. It is reasonable to develop further the talent that one's father or grandfather worked hard at and not switch to something entirely new; otherwise, one is depriving himself of the chance to attain perfection in some one craft. Thus, the saying 'which street should you take? – that of your ancestors'[2]

Jung, who had listened attentively, turned to face Nietzsche and said,

I have become aware of the fateful links between me and my ancestors. I feel very strongly that I am under the influence of things or questions which were left incomplete and that I have to answer or solve these questions on behalf of my ancestors as it were. These might well be my personal questions too, but, on the other hand, if a collective problem isn't recognized as such it can only be experienced as a personal one. This to me means, I have no other street to choose from, so to say.

Nietzsche remained standing for a moment in acknowledgment and appreciation of Jung's words, before sitting again.

Meanwhile, Rilke had prepared himself to say something, just a few words. Lou saw his attempt and burst forth such loving breathtaking feeling to Rilke, her 15 years' younger lover, that, while Inayat Khan looked down at his lap, Jung's curiosity was stirred and he quietly reflected in his mind, "He was right sometimes, Freud. When he said, 'Lou is both his muse and attentive mother,'[3] there was something to it."

Encouraged, although still hesitant, Rilke stood, weighing at first from one foot to another, then squarely facing Lou, extemporizing, "You are the future, the red dawn that your ancestors could only dream of, but whose light they nonetheless carried in their hearts."[4]

Jung, reading the room, returned to the exercise and said,

Connecting with the elements, which are inherently pure, seems to transmit their sense of vitality – of life itself – as though life itself were realigned within me. It reminded me of my experiments with Kundalini yoga and its capacity to calm the psyche. Breath truly bridges the unconscious and conscious realms.

Inayat Khan responded,

Breath is not only life's essence but the bridge between the material and the spiritual. It has the power to transform and elevate consciousness. Through its rhythm it creates harmony within the self and aligns us with the universe. This is why, in mysticism, we often say, 'Breath is the soul of practice'.

Jung thoughtfully nodded.

Fascinating. I have always been drawn to practices that link the body and the psyche. Breathing, as you describe it, aligns with what I have observed in my patients – a natural rhythm of psyche and soma. It seems to me that this practice mirrors the processes of individuation. Integration and harmony often begin with the simplest of actions, such as breathing or even drawing a spontaneous mandala.

Inayat Khan: "Exactly. The simplest practices often contain the deepest wisdom. The breath connects the elements within us – earth, water, fire, air, and ether. Each element represents a state of being, and when they are in balance, we achieve harmony."

Jung, contemplating his experience followed a thought, "Breathwork is *not yet* part of Western psychoanalytical treatment, but I am certain it will find its way there in time."

Inayat Khan continued,

Breath, you see, is the essence of attunement. It harmonizes body and soul and facilitates the awareness necessary for transformation. But breath alone is only one aspect. In our tradition, we also use the repetition of sacred words, a practice that deepens awareness and raises consciousness.

Then paused to explain further,

These sacred words – passed down from teacher to pupil – are imbued with a resonance that transcends language. Whether in Arabic, Persian, or Hindustani, the words serve as a vehicle for spiritual ascent. They unify the seeker's inner and outer worlds.

Jung,

That resonates deeply. Unity, I've found, originates from maintaining awareness within the unconscious – a sort of inner attunement. Often, in analysis, I sense layers of voices within a patient's psyche: the echoes of parents, ancestors, even collective archetypes. It can feel overwhelming, a veritable cacophony. Yet, through quiet observation – what you call 'quietism' – a resolution often emerges. Silent transference can guide the resolution of complexes that might otherwise resist verbal confrontation, only tightening their grip on the patient. It's not always spoken but felt.

Inayat Khan, continued,

Indeed, quietude reveals the path. In Sufism, the relationship between the teacher and pupil – what we call the Murshid and the *mureed* – is one of trust. The Murshid illuminates the way, through the uncharted terrain toward self-realization, offering guidance through experience rather than instruction. But the Murshid himself also receives guidance – through initiation into the *silsila*, the chain of transmission that connects every teacher to the lineage of all who came before.

The process of purification through the *nafs* – the different concepts of self, or egos – forms the foundation of Sufi philosophy and psychology.

The first stage is *nafs al-Amara*. It represents self-centered passions that drive a person's actions without concern for others. Then there is *nafs al-Luwama*, the self-blaming mind. At this stage, one moves toward indifference to others' opinions – whether approval or disapproval. Such external validation becomes irrelevant, as it is seen as detrimental to spiritual development. The third stage, *nafs al-Mutmainna*, brings peace, ease, and contentment. Mental purification and the practice of *zikr*, the remembrance of God, become crucial at this stage. Whether through prayers, prostrations, breath, or repetitions; all of these practices support the journey through the successive states of the *nafs*.

This way, by gradually shedding, time and again, every day, more and more aspects of the *nafs*, the false self, we come closer to the true Self. And to God.

Jung looked up slightly, reminiscing,

That reminds me of a patient and her approach during analysis. She persisted in prayer, engaging with archetypal figures through creative fantasy – a process not unlike samskara. She used this as a means to understand herself and her personal myth. The unconscious serves as the medium for religious experiences. Individuation, similarly, begins when the Self separates itself from the ego, its passions and entanglements. This detachment leads to the experience of the numinous – call it God or not – a presence that needs no rational verification. It is a freeing of the soul, allowing it to express itself authentically. This is what ultimately leads to wholeness.

Inayat Khan, his voice tinged with curiosity, added, "Ah, what you are describing is deeply interesting."

Jung nodded, his expression thoughtful, "A very recognizable process – it has a universal quality to it."

Jung sat back, stroking his chin as if weighing his words. Then, with a deliberate pause, he said,

Hmm . . . To me, it sounds like for you, self-realization is a process that moves upward – up, up, up. He gestured with his hand, tracing an invisible ascent in the air.

For me, individuation also involves moving downward – down, down, down, his voice deepened, and outward – to the left and to the right.

The room was silent, all eyes on him. He leaned in, his expression intent.

You see, in my view, the small self, essentially the ego, is fully encircled by the Self on all fronts. The Self dwells in the unconscious, while the ego, as the conscious part of the whole person, naturally believes it is the 'only one,' because it does not – and cannot – automatically acknowledge what it is unconscious of.

He paused, letting his words settle. Then, thoughtfully connecting his point to Hazrat Inayat Khan's earlier description, he said,

The true Self . . . and the false self, you say. I have been pondering this polarity for a long time. Are these truly opposites? If so, how can one live within a field charged by such opposing forces?

Jung allowed the question to hang in the air. Then, with a wry smile, he added,

The Jungians – thank God I am Jung and not 'a Jungian' – herald the cliché of reconciling the opposites as though it were merely a method for muddling through. But what does that really mean? This is what most people do not endeavor to fully realize, and I can explain why.

His tone became more animated, and he began to speak with greater urgency:

Firstly, coming to terms with inner conflict depends on a non-rational, non-conceptual, and non-premeditated attitude. This is not a process one can think one's way through. Secondly, he continued, his eyes now scanning the audience, it takes massive courage to acknowledge the presence of something within – and even around oneself – that one cannot comprehend. The Self is not a thing to be grasped, it is an 'other' – an unknown force. And yet, there is an instinctual dependency on it, combined with the urge to break free, to win freedom from it – not through willing surrender, but through a kind of imagined victory over the Self. Just imagine that!

He laughed softly, as if marveling at the oxymoron. His voice too had softened as he went on.

These are the reasons why most fail to reconcile the opposites within themselves. But for those who do . . . those who are lucky enough to encounter this reality . . . there comes a knowing. This knowing is irreversible. It propels one into bewilderment, confusion, and . . . a certain loneliness. A loneliness shared with the other within.

The atmosphere grew charged, the weight of his words palpable.

At this stage, the conflict is no longer a battle between two adversaries – a fist-fight, man to man, or a struggle to see who will come out on top. No. It transforms into something else entirely: a tension between two inner forces that long to unite. This, Jung emphasized, "is the inexplicable paradox."

He hesitated, then, banging one hand on his chest, his voice dropping to a near whisper.

It is an experience . . . very deep . . .

His words trailed off, as though nevertheless searching for the fathomable.

Hazrat Inayat Khan, who had been listening intently, bent towards Jung, their faces now mere inches apart, and whispered, "Yes?"

Jung's eyes glittered with intensity. His voice suddenly firm and rapid.

It is an experience that turns into knowing – first of the nature of the other within, and then of the intimate relationship between the two. Their collaboration, their embeddedness within the Self – the higher Self. And where else would the higher Self be but embedded in itself? And in God, in nature, in the cosmos . . . in all that is. That, he declared, is what I mean.

The room seemed to hold its breath. Then, with a quiet certainty, Jung concluded,

This objective knowing is the essence of the *coniunctio*. The alchemists described the Self as an indissoluble substance – an indivisible, united One. The *filius macrocosmi*. One is what one always was and ever will become. Growth emerges from the limitless unconscious, and yet it remains an individual endeavor. This is what I have called the individuation process – a journey that I see not only as a personal path but as an ethical principle. For in essence, individuation is your contribution – your personal contribution – to the entirety of consciousness.

Jung sat up straighter, his posture firming as though he were collecting himself. When he spoke again, his tone shifted, taking on a more didactic quality.

This lifelong journey of individuation, Jung began, his voice measured and thoughtful, is not something one can think one's way through. The unconscious doesn't respond to logic or reasoning – it speaks in symbols, images, and feelings. To truly engage with it, one must learn to listen and respond in its own language. It is a process that moves through various sensory states – whether in dreams, spontaneous mandalas, or even dance. This is especially true for the natural process of individuation. But in the context of analysis, there is one indispensable practice for fostering individuation: Active Imagination.

He glanced around the room, pausing to let his words sink in. His tone grew deliberate, as though inviting the audience to grasp the weight of what he was about to share.

For this journey, we need a practice – a way to enter into dialogue with the depths of the psyche. In my work, I have called this active imagination: a method that bridges the conscious and unconscious, enabling a collaboration that brings forth the Self in all its richness. He leaned forward slightly, as if to draw everyone in.

Firstly, its purpose is to create a living bridge between the personal unconscious and personal consciousness. This includes interacting with images emerging from the unconscious, whether subjective or objective, as well as engaging with archetypes of the collective unconscious.
    Although it has dreamlike qualities, active imagination is consciously practiced. This allows waking consciousness to actively witness and interact with the autonomous unconscious, creating a unique space for integration.

Secondly, the process unfolds in stages. Initially, one lets the unconscious take the lead while the witnessing consciousness observes. In the second stage, consciousness takes the lead. This is the most significant phase, as it involves grappling with questions of meaning and moral demands. All aspects of an issue are laid out, allowing differences to be observed and resolved. This dynamic exchange leads to transformation – a deeply intrapsychic process rooted in the unconscious.

Inayat Khan, listening well, inclined his head. "I see," he said, weighing his response.

But before I comment, I must emphasize that for me, there is no 'up, up, up' possible at all unless a *mureed* is first firmly grounded in their own psychology. I make it a point to assess their ability to remain intact in the face of the tests I expose them to. This grounding is an essential part of the training I offer, undertaken with great responsibility, before I introduce any practices of ascension. Now, what you say about active imagination is very interesting and quite distinct from the Sufi process of purification and transformation through the *nafs*. While Sufis actively engage in this journey, we recognize that the ultimate realization *comes* only by the grace of God. Our approach to Creative Imagination differs as well. Its purpose is to unite with the image and to know its nature from within. The contemplator becomes the contemplated through direct communion and divine revelation.

Inayat Khan paused and gauged Jung's silent response before continuing,

The *Alam al-Mithal*, the world of images, is a universe that exists as an intermediary between God and manifestation. It is as real as the manifest world, inhabited by subtle bodies, *jinns,* angels, and even some minds of the departed. This realm is one plane of unification. Ultimately, we arrive at the same point of *coniunctio* – the unity of opposites, *coincidentia oppositorum:* consciousness merging with the unconscious; Spirit harmonizing with body, mind, and heart.

At this moment, Lou, shifted slightly in her chair and cast a discreet glance at her watch. Her subtle signal brought instant silence from both men, who exchanged an unspoken understanding.

After a brief pause, Jung tapped his pipe thoughtfully, meeting Inayat Khan's eye. "But let's not leave without saying a few words on love – and the *coniunctio*."

Inayat Khan held his gaze, nodding encouragingly.

Jung, "Allow me to start," he offered as he turned to Lou, then faced the audience directly.

Personally, I could not continue living one day without the woman, although, at times, I fear her and find it difficult to live with her. I share in the famous conundrum: 'What does a woman want?' And often, I haven't the faintest idea.

But I have learned, and sometimes mastered, how to fulfill the needs of the women in my life – just as they have fulfilled mine. Marie-Louise, Sabina, Toni . . . Women have been indispensable for both my career and my emotional growth. They have played a vital role in my journey to the anima, their presence mirroring paths that led me deeper into myself.

Especially my wife, Emma. She has been my steadfast companion throughout everything. Jung's expression softened as he seemed to turn inward for a moment. "You know," he began,

Emma's individuation process was far less dramatic than mine – less marked by the terror, labor, and relentless confrontation with the unconscious that has so often defined my own journey. Yet, hers was no less profound, no less fully accomplished. In her case, it was through enduring love, a steadfastness of the heart, and an ability to hold the tension of opposites with grace. She became, in so many ways, my anchor – a living embodiment of the principles we both sought to understand. Our deep union was confirmed to me after her death – in a dream, though it felt more like a vision. She appeared to me in her prime, standing tall and looking directly at me. She wore a dress – perhaps her most beautiful one – and her expression was neutral, yet objectively wise and deeply understanding. There was no trace of emotional reaction, as if she stood beyond the haze of earthly moves. In that vision, I saw the entirety of our 53 years of marriage: its beginning, the events of our life together, and the end of her time here. Confronted with such completeness, one is rendered speechless – it defies comprehension.

Inayat Khan rested respectfully in his chair before speaking,

Women have undoubtedly been a treasured source of vision and consolation in my life as well. My mother, especially, who I adored and cherished beyond measure. The union of our hearts was so profound that even physical distance could not diminish it.

I remember vividly a time when I was quite young and away from home for the first time. I was climbing a mountain in Nepal with my father and fell, injuring my knee. That night, in a dream – though truly, it felt like a vision – my mother appeared. She tended to my knee, comforting me with her presence. Later, I learned that she had dreamt of me showing her my wounded knee. Her spirit had transcended distance to care for me.

Throughout my life, I have found my mother's spirit reflected in the women who have supported my work and family. These collaborators have been indispensable, particularly in my efforts in the West, and I hold immense gratitude for them.

Inayat Khan paused, his expression contemplative. "There are authentic stories from India of men who have undertaken the forty days of seclusion, spending most of their time immersed in *zikr*. In such states, they often become overwhelmed by a heightened sensual awareness, which explains the many erotic metaphors used to describe union with the Beloved – with God, who is love, harmony, and beauty. . . . The physical senses serve as a royal road to perceiving both the external and internal worlds. The signs of God may manifest in anything – a stone, a flower, an animal, a fragrance, or a most beautiful woman. The highest spiritual experience may well come through the senses themselves."

The room fell still. Some exchanged glances, others studied their hands and nails, the grain of the table, the floor. A few chairs scraped lightly against the wood. Then, after a moment's pause, Lou rose.

She turned first to Inayat Khan, inclining her head slightly in gratitude. Reaching into her bag, she withdrew a thin collection of papers, carefully bound, and handed them to him. "Just a few poems of mine," she said softly. "I thank you from my heart."

Inayat Khan bowed in return, accepting the gift with quiet grace.

Lou stepped back toward her chair, picked up a thick notebook, and turned to Jung. She stretched out her arms as if in an embrace, then, with a knowing smile, presented it to him with both hands. "Some thoughts on why life is worth living after all," she said. "Thank you ever so much for being here with us today."

A wave of applause rippled through the room, warm and appreciative. Lou turned, addressing everyone. "And now, I want to thank all of you for being here. It is time for refreshments. Please, follow me."

Notes

1 This chapter draws upon and adapts material from the works of Carl Jung and Hazrat Inayat Khan. While no direct quotations are used, the ideas and concepts are inspired by the following major works: From C.G. Jung: *Memories, Dreams, Reflections*, Vol. 268 (Vintage, 1963); *C.G. Jung Letters*, Vol. II, 2 vols. (Princeton University Press, 1989); *Mysterium Coniunctionis: An Inquiry into the Separation and Synthesis of Psychic Opposites in Alchemy* (Princeton University Press, 1963); *The Structure and Dynamics of the Psyche, Vol. 8 of The Collected Works of C.G. Jung* (Princeton University Press, 1969); *The Freud-Jung Letters: The Correspondence Between Sigmund Freud and C.G. Jung* (Princeton University Press, 1974); *The Red Book: Liber Novus*; "Concerning Rebirth," in *The Archetypes and the Collective Unconscious, Collected Works*, Vol. 9.1, paras.

199–258; and *Reflections on the Life and Dreams of C.G. Jung*, by Aniela Jaffé, translated by Caitlin Stephens, with commentary by Elena Fischli (Daimon Verlag; Princeton University Press, 2023). From Hazrat Inayat Khan: *The Mysticism of Sound and Music* (Motilal Banarsidass, 1974); *The Story of My Mystical Life*; *The Biography of Pir-o-Murshid Inayat Khan* (London and The Hague: East-West Publications, 1979); *The Sufi Message*, Volume 12: *Confessions: Autobiographical Essays of Hazrat Inayat Khan: The Early Years*; and *Metaphysics: The Experience of the Soul in Different Planes of Existence*, Volume 5 of *The Sufi Message*.

2 Friedrich Nietzsche, *Human, All Too Human: A Book for Free Spirits*, trans. Marion Faber and Stephen Lehmann (Lincoln: University of Nebraska Press, 1984).

3 Though not found verbatim in Freud's writings, this remark has often been attributed to him in biographical discussions of Rilke and Lou Andreas-Salomé. See: Ralph Freedman, *Life of a Poet: Rainer Maria Rilke* (Evanston: Northwestern University Press, 1996), 163–165.

4 Rainer Maria Rilke, *The Book of Pilgrimage, Vol. 2 of The Book of Hours*, trans. Babette Deutsch (New York: New Directions Publishing, 1941).

Chapter 8

Convergence and Divergence at the Suez Delta

Introduction

Jung at the Threshold: Between Science and the Numinous

Carl Jung was born into a world shaped by traditional Christianity and Protestant rationalism – a framework he would later reinterpret through his exhaustive studies of Gnosticism, alchemy, symbolism, and the religions of both West and East. He never professed a faith of his own but remained deeply intrigued by, and respectful of, all religions.

His life evolved at the intersection of two opposing currents: the scientific and the mystical, the rational and the numinous. From early on, he was aware of these dual influences expressed in *Memories, Dreams, Reflections* as his two person-alities: the empirical, scientifically minded researcher (Personality #1)[1] and the timeless, intuitive observer of the unseen (Personality #2). His family background reinforced this tension. His mother had two distinct personalities, his grandfather reportedly spoke with the spirit of his deceased wife, and his cousin was a practic-ing medium. Spirit phenomena were not abstract concepts to Jung; they were part of his lived reality. And yet, rather than simply succumbing to the mystical pull of his ancestry, he sought to bridge these worlds, engaging with the irrational while remaining rooted in psychological inquiry.

Throughout his life, Jung maintained an ongoing dialogue with the unseen, whether through his encounters with inner figures, his explorations of alchemy and the collective unconscious, or his transmission of *Seven Sermons to the Dead*, a moment of profound inner revelation. He accepted the reality of such experiences, yet he worked to translate them into psychological language, fitting them within the intellectual framework of his time. His concept of the *unus mundus* – the idea of a unified underlying reality where psyche and matter are one – illustrates this synthesis.[2] While deeply resonant with mystical traditions from Neoplatonism to Sufism, Jung treated it with the cautious reverence of a scientific mystic, committed to rigorous inquiry while acknowledging the limits of reductionist explanations.

Jung's balancing act between empirical rigor and openness to mystical experi-ence places him in the same intellectual stream as William James, whose *Varieties*

DOI: 10.4324/9781003431336-8

of Religious Experience deeply influenced his thinking. Like James, Jung resisted the binary between scientific materialism and religious dogma, instead seeking to understand mystical and psychic experiences phenomenologically, that is, on their own terms rather than through preconceived theoretical frameworks. Both men were pioneers of a psychology that took subjective experience seriously without discarding scientific scrutiny, and both were instrumental in shaping a vision of consciousness that was neither purely mechanistic nor entirely esoteric.

His near-death experience in 1944 further intensified this convergence. It did not lead him to abandon the scientific rigor of his earlier works, but it did deepen his willingness to incorporate the numinous more explicitly into his psychology. The shift was subtle but significant: Jung no longer merely analyzed mystical experiences; he recognized their undeniable truth. In his final opus, *Mysterium Coniunctionis*, he articulated the sacred union of opposites as not just a psychological necessity but an encounter with the deepest layers of being.

Jung was neither a mystic in the traditional sense nor a reductionist scientist. He stood at the threshold, refusing to collapse one reality into the other. It is precisely this paradox – the attempt to hold together rational inquiry and direct experience of the numinous – that makes his work so vital today. In an age caught between the sterility of scientism and the excesses of unchecked mysticism, Jung's model offers a way forward: an integration of the empirical and the ineffable, the analytic and the intuitive.

Inayat Khan at the Threshold: Between East and West

Born into a devoted Muslim household in Baroda, India, Hazrat Inayat Khan was raised in an environment of deep spiritual devotion, artistic refinement, and intellectual inquiry. Though firmly rooted in Sufi mysticism, his family embraced a broad cultural and philosophical openness. This unique fusion of tradition and openness shaped Inayat Khan's path, enabling him to become a bridge between East and West and a translator of ancient Eastern wisdom into modern Western language.

Music was the heartbeat of this world. For Inayat Khan, music was as much a sacred practice as a scientific discipline, and one that shaped his early understanding of the universe. As a child prodigy in classical Indian music, he learned to perceive sound as the language of the soul, a bridge between the material and the unseen. This early exposure to vibrational essence would later inform his entire mystical vision, as well as his understanding of the human psyche.

Despite his immersion in the spiritual and artistic life of India, Inayat Khan was called beyond its borders. When he received the inner command to bring Sufism to the West, he stepped into a world vastly different from the one that had shaped him. The rationalist, fragmented mentality of the West, so focused on analysis and external mastery, stood in stark contrast to the Sufi view of knowledge as an opening of the heart, a journey of attunement rather than intellectual conquest. Yet, rather than rejecting this world, he dedicated himself to translation by conceptually adapting the timeless principles of Sufi cosmology into a language that could be grasped by Western seekers. His Sufism was based on his living transmission through sound, music, and words.

Inayat Khan was part of a broader intellectual and spiritual movement that sought to unify Eastern and Western wisdom, much like his contemporary Swami Vivekananda, who introduced Vedanta to Western audiences, or Ralph Waldo Emerson, whose transcendentalist writings echoed the themes of universal spirituality. His work also resonates with Rudolf Steiner's vision of an esoteric Christianity that integrates mystical insight with practical wisdom. Like these men, Inayat Khan saw no contradiction between inner realization and engagement with the psychic world. Instead, long before transpersonal psychology emerged as a field, he articulated a vision in which psychology and mysticism were closely intertwined. He understood the psyche as an instrument to be tuned and refined through purification, deepened through love, and ultimately harmonized with the divine. The path of the heart was central to his teaching, as was the understanding that consciousness itself was not a fixed state but a spectrum, ascending through stages of awakening.

Unlike Jung, Inayat Khan did not frame his work within the language of scientific discourse, but his approach shared a striking similarity: he was both a mystic and a methodical observer of the inner life. He remained fully immersed in the mystical vision of divine love while offering a structured path toward self-realization. His Western students, unfamiliar with the fluid and symbolic nature of Sufi wisdom, often required explanations that met them where they were. And so, he tirelessly reinterpreted, making the invisible accessible, the mystical tangible. This ceaseless adaptation was his way of service, his surrender to the divine presence, which he considered all-pervading.

Inayat Khan's life was brief, yet his impact was lasting. He never saw himself as a religious reformer, nor did he seek institutional authority. Instead, he worked joyfully and unwaveringly, serving only God, his mission carried by devotion rather than personal ambition. His death at the age of 44 marked the end of his physical presence, but his work continues through his writings, through his music, and through the silent transmission of those who have walked the path he illuminated.

In an age still divided between the analytic and the mystical, the structured and the intuitive, Inayat Khan's legacy offers a reminder: knowledge of the soul cannot be confined to one tradition, one language, or one way of knowing. Like music, it moves through different keys and rhythms, always seeking harmony, always seeking to return to its source.

Convergence and Divergence in Perspective

The meeting of Carl Jung and Hazrat Inayat Khan's philosophies offers a unique opportunity to explore the profound ways in which psychology and mysticism approach the human experience. While each thinker walked distinct paths – Jung rooted primarily in the analytical framework of the Western psyche, and Inayat

Khan steeped in the spiritual and devotional tradition of the Chishti Sufism of India – their shared focus on human transformation reveals striking points of convergence. Both sought to illuminate the inner workings of the Self and soul, and to guide individuals toward a higher state of consciousness, albeit through different methods, languages, and cultural lenses.

Understanding where their ideas align and where they diverge is essential not only for appreciating the richness of their respective contributions but also for uncovering new insights at the intersection of psychology and spirituality. This chapter explores how their approaches overlap and contrast across foundational themes, from dreams and imagination to the ego-self dynamic and the ultimate goal of human development. By examining these convergences and divergences, we uncover the deeper significance of their work as a combined map for navigating the complexities of self-realization and individuation.

Their Views on Themselves

Both men saw themselves as pioneers navigating uncharted territories of human consciousness. They shared a profound sense of purpose, each dedicated to guiding individuals toward a deeper understanding of themselves and the world.[3]

Jung's work was rooted in Western science and psychology, positioning him as a bridge between the rational framework of modernity and the irrational forces of the psyche he sought to recover. Hazrat Inayat Khan, in contrast, drew upon centuries-old Sufi spiritual traditions, presenting himself as a bridge between East and West. Jung's engagement with the psyche was often characterized by struggle and confrontation, reflecting his focus on integrating opposites within the individual. Inayat Khan's approach, however, centered on harmony and love, emphasizing surrender and the transcendence of duality.

Methodology, Language, and Culture

While their goals align, the methodologies and the languages of Carl Jung and Inayat Khan, shaped by their respective fields and cultural influences, diverge significantly.

Jung, emerging from early 20th-century Europe, grappled with crises of modernity such as the loss of faith, the rise of industrialization, and the shadow of war. His work sought to restore meaning in a disenchanted world, emphasizing the individuation process as a response to the fragmentation of modern life in search of soul. Jung's approach, rooted in the scientific and empirical framework of Western psychology, emphasized structured methods such as dream analysis and active imagination. He delved into archetypes and the collective unconscious, employing precise and analytical language that resonated with his audience of scholars and clinicians.

Inayat Khan, rooted in the mystical traditions of the East, approached self-realization as a universal ideal, transcending the boundaries of culture and creed.

His mission to bring his Sufi Message to the West reflected his belief in the unity of all religious ideals, a perspective shaped by his upbringing in India and his immersion in the Chishti Order. While Jung often focused on the individual's journey into the collective unconscious, Inayat Khan placed equal emphasis on the collective engagement with the unconscious, envisioning a world harmonized by love, beauty, and spiritual liberty.

While Jung relied on the rigor of intellect and analysis, Inayat Khan appealed to the intuitive and the experiential knowing of the heart, inviting his followers to dissolve boundaries rather than analyze them. Inayat Khan's teachings drew upon Sufi mysticism, where the path to self-realization is marked by the subtleties of the heart, the refinement of the breath, and the resonance of music. His teachings were no less systematic than Jung's, yet often conveyed through narrative legends, metaphors, and poetry that transcend rational explanation.

Given the distinct methodologies and languages Jung and Inayat Khan employed in their teachings, it becomes evident that these approaches are deeply influenced by their cultural and historical contexts. The environments in which they lived not only shaped their perspectives but also framed the challenges they sought to address, revealing key divergences in their understanding of the self and the world.

Dreams

One key aspect of their shared understanding of the inner landscape is the realm of dreams. For Jung, dreams were vital tools for psychological insight and individuation, while for Inayat Khan, they may serve as occasional windows into higher realms of spiritual guidance.

For Jung, dreams were messages from the unconscious, guiding the individuation process and offering insight into personal and universal truths. Similarly, Inayat Khan acknowledged that certain dreams, for instance, those in which divine messages are given in letters or by an angelic voice, could convey one's inner psychological and spiritual states.

Jung placed dreams at the center of his psychological framework and developed a systematic approach to uncover and interpret the unconscious material embedded within them. In contrast, Inayat Khan, while recognizing the spiritual significance of some dreams, did not emphasize dream interpretation as a structured method for self-realization, focusing instead on devotional practices and direct, waking spiritual experience.

The Role of Imagination

From the symbolic language of dreams, we move naturally to another shared yet distinct focus: imagination. Both men saw imagination not at all as fantasy but rather as a most vital bridge between the material and spiritual realms, offering profound possibilities for transformation.

For Jung, imagination was the medium through which the unconscious communicates and interacts with the conscious mind. Jung's method of *active imagination* requires sustained inner engagement with images, figures, and moods arising from the unconscious. As the practitioner listens with open curiosity, responds to the object of the inner dialogue, and integrates insights, synchronicities in daily life may occur as a result of such active connection with the unconscious. Inayat Khan, too, saw imagination as central to the spiritual journey, though his perspective was steeped in the metaphysical. He described the *"Alam al-Mithal,"* as a plane of existence that mediates between the divine and the manifest. Through *creative imagination* and meditative practices, he encouraged his disciples to unite with these images and figures, and ultimately to achieve an intimate communion with the divine. Inayat Khan emphasized *attunement* as a practice preparing for creative imagination by means of music, breath, silence, and *zikr*.

Archetypes and Symbols

Hence, imagination, for both Jung and Inayat Khan, serves as a transformative bridge between the material and spiritual realms. Yet, the images and visions encountered through imagination do not exist in isolation; they are part of a greater tapestry of universal patterns and meanings. Archetypes and symbols provide a language through which these deeper truths are expressed.

Jung's fascination with archetypes finds a natural resonance with Inayat Khan's use of symbols. Both saw these as universal expressions of the human psyche and soul, though their interpretations differed. For Jung, archetypes were innate patterns that emerge from the collective unconscious, providing a framework for understanding the human experience. Inayat Khan viewed symbols as reflections of divine reality, offering glimpses into the spiritual truths that underlie existence.

The figure of Khidr, for instance, emerges as a shared symbol in their work. Jung encountered Khidr as an archetype of guidance in his active imagination, while Inayat Khan revered Khidr as the mystical guide who appears at moments of spiritual initiation. Though their interpretations were colored by their respective traditions, both recognized Khidr's role as a bridge between the known and the unknown, the earthly and the divine. Khidr is also frequently – though not without controversy – understood to be among the four immortal prophets, alongside Enoch, Elijah, and Jesus.

The Journey of Individuation and Self-Realization

For both men, this journey – whether termed individuation or self-realization – was a profound process of becoming, marked by inner struggle, self-discovery, and an encounter with something greater than the limited self. They also agreed on the necessity of embracing the unknown. Their approaches to this journey, however, reveal a salient interplay of convergence and divergence. Jung's individuation process was centered on integration of opposites, of unconscious material, of archetypal energies. It was deeply individualistic. In contrast, Inayat Khan's self-realization involved surrender to the divine and the experience of unity with all existence, moving beyond individual concerns.

In both, consciousness develops not through conceptual mastery, but through opening, listening, and relating to it.

The archetypes and symbols that both Jung and Inayat Khan revered point toward deeper dynamics within the psyche and the soul. Central to their teachings is the interplay between the ego and the larger Self and soul, a relationship that reflects the struggle and aspiration at the heart of human transformation. Both men grappled with this tension, though their interpretations and approaches reveal significant contrasts.

Jung saw the ego as a necessary structure for navigating the world, emphasizing its integration with the unconscious rather than its dissolution. Inayat Khan, however, emphasized purification and effacement of the ego to align fully with God's will, reflecting his Sufi ideals. In both, the ego is not eliminated but refined, becoming transparent to something deeper and more universal. Each path recognized that the psyche is not a closed system but open to symbolic, transpersonal, and transformative dimensions.

Guidance, too, remains essential. Jung discovered autonomous inner figures. His engagement with figures like Philemon and Salome illustrates the psyche's capacity to generate inner teachers that mediate transformation and oriented him toward psychospiritual wholeness. Inayat Khan, while grounded in a living initiatic tradition, points toward the same function: a *Murshid,* not a source of authority in the conventional sense, but a mirror in which the seeker perceives what lies dormant within as well as a link to the *silsila,* the chain of initiates that have preceded the *Murshid* in the same Sufi lineage. In Jungian terminology, one might envision the *silsila* as a distinct "stream" in the collective unconscious. In both cases, whether conceived as inner archetype or outer guide, the function remains to orient consciousness toward its higher attainment. Guidance serves to orient consciousness toward what Jung called the Self and Inayat Khan named God.

Moreover, both affirm that development takes place within the tension of opposites. Jung's process of *enantiodromia* – the psyche's need to reconcile opposing tendencies that emerge in the course of time – is mirrored in Inayat Khan's understanding of balance between inner and outer, form and essence, silence and sound. Consciousness matures through the capacity to contain and transmute polarities, not through avoidance of contradiction. Considered through the lens of consciousness development, their underlying structures reveal key points of convergence. Both offer a rigorous path toward transformation, grounded in lived experience and sustained effort.

Ultimately, what sets both approaches apart is their shared insistence that transformation is not an abstract ideal. Carl Jung and Inayat Khan, each in their own way, outline an empirically grounded, experientially tested path toward inner coherence. Theirs are paths that welcome suffering as incentives for growth, encourage full participation in the world, and offer substantial roadmaps for chartering the inner, immaterial life. They suggest that higher consciousness is not generally given. It may, however, be cultivated through devotion, through symbolic engagement, through facing one's inner depths, and through the gradual orientation of one's whole being toward that which the soul experiences as most real and true at any given point in time.

What unites these two systems is this shared affirmation: development of consciousness is attainable. It is not reserved for saints or mystics, nor confined to theoretical discourse. It is a structured, experiential process of refinement and awakening. Individuation and self-realization are movements from fragmentation to coherence, from opacity to inner clarity. Carl Jung and Inayat Khan offer distinct but complementary maps for this process, grounded in attention to imagination, love, and the discipline of the inner life.

Experiences Through the Senses and in Nature

Both Carl Jung and Inayat Khan saw the senses and the natural world as essential gateways to higher consciousness. For each, sensory experience opened access to the archetypal, the numinous, and the divine.

Jung's connection to nature – his time in the Alps or by the lake at Bollingen – anchored his inner work. These encounters stirred archetypal resonance and grounded his personal myth. For him, nature was closely associated with the unconscious, erupting in signs and synchronicities that marked the path of individuation – "the Kingfisher encounter" being but one example hereof.

In contrast, Inayat Khan regarded the senses, especially hearing, as devotional instruments. Sound, for him, expressed the divine directly through the "music of the spheres." Nature was not symbolic but sacred in itself, a mirror of God's presence.

Both men were deeply attuned to the numinous: that overwhelming sense of the holy which escapes rational grasp. Jung found it in dreams, active imagination, and spontaneous artwork. Inayat Khan encountered it in mystical union, music, and *zikr*, remembrance of God.

Yet their orientations diverged. For Jung, the numinous, in essence, bridged the conscious and unconscious, revealing psychic wholeness. For Inayat Khan, it was a direct embodiment of the divine realized through love, surrender, and devotion.

Their Visions of the Soul

Both Jung and Inayat Khan regarded the soul as central to the human journey of transformation. For Jung, the soul was a dynamic entity, partly unconscious. In *The Red Book*, he described his dialogues with the soul as essential to navigating the depths of the unconscious and fostering integration, a process central to individuation. Similarly, Inayat Khan saw the soul as the essence of divine reality, describing it as a "ray of the sun" that is not separate from its source, the infinite spirit. Like Jung, he acknowledged the soul's role as a guiding force, leading the seeker toward unity with the infinite.

While Jung often conceptualized the soul symbolically – particularly through archetypes like the anima and animus that mediate between the conscious and unconscious – or in the form of mandalas, Inayat Khan's vision of the soul was metaphysical and devotional. He emphasized the unity between God and the soul, inseparable, yet appearing distinct. For Inayat Khan, the soul's journey was not about reconciling opposites or integrating unconscious material, as in Jung's individuation process, but about realizing its inherent unity with the divine and surrendering to that oneness.

The Ultimate Goal

From their visions of the soul as a guiding force, we arrive at the question of where this journey ultimately leads. For both Jung and Inayat Khan, the culmination of the inner journey holds profound significance, though their conceptions of the ultimate goal diverge in ways that reveal the core of their respective teachings.

Perhaps the most profound divergence between Jung and Inayat Khan lies in their conception of the ultimate goal of the inner journey. For Jung, individuation is a psychological process that leads to a state of wholeness. While he acknowledges the numinous and the spiritual as important elements in the individuation process, his framework remains grounded in the psyche's development.

Inayat Khan, on the other hand, envisions self-realization as a state of divine consciousness, where the individual soul merges with the universal soul. His teachings transcend the psychological, pointing toward a mystical union with God that lies beyond the limits of human understanding. For Inayat Khan, the journey does not end with the Self but dissolves into the infinite.

The Delta: Where Waters Meet

While their ultimate goals reflect the profound divergence at the heart of their teachings, Jung and Inayat Khan share a deep commitment to guiding humanity toward transformation. Their perspectives – one rooted in the integration of the psyche, the other in union with the divine – offer harmonizing insights into the human journey. At their meeting point, we find the possibility of synthesis, where their legacies flow together like rivers converging into a vast, shared ocean.

The convergence and divergence of Jung and Inayat Khan at the metaphorical Suez Delta reveal the richness of their legacies. Together, they offer complementary pathways for understanding the human experience – one rooted in the depths of the psyche, the other in the heights of the spirit. Their dialogue invites us to embrace both perspectives, recognizing that the journey inward is as much a psychological endeavor as it is a spiritual quest.

In this meeting of minds, we find not only the interplay of differences but the possibility of integration – a reminder that the path to wholeness is both deeply personal and a collective endeavor.

Notes

1 Carl G. Jung, *Memories, Dreams, Reflections*, ed. Aniela Jaffé, trans. Richard and Clara Winston (New York: Vintage, 1989), 44–45.
2 Jung, *Memories, Dreams, Reflections*, 279.
3 It is worth noting that both men sustained lifelong marriages with women who whole-heartedly supported their vocations. Emma Jung not only stood by Carl Jung during his psychological crises and explorations, but also became an accomplished analyst and writer in her own right. Her work on the Grail legend and on the animus contributed meaningfully to analytical psychology. Similarly, Pirani Ameena Begum played a vital role in Hazrat Inayat Khan's spiritual mission, embodying and articulating elements of his teachings through hospitality. For both men, the marital bond was a private partnership in service of their respective causes and a larger spiritual or psychological vision.

Chapter 9

Carl Jung and Inayat Khan in a World in Crisis

In the first decades of the 20th century, when Carl Gustav Jung and Hazrat Inayat Khan were formulating the foundations of their life's work, the world was marked by collapsing empires, technological acceleration, and growing spiritual uncertainty. The atmosphere was saturated with both dread and anticipation and created a cultural mood of moral decline and existential questioning. The unprecedented trauma of World War I, the devastation of the 1918 pandemic, and the redrawing of borders in its aftermath seeded long-lasting geopolitical and psychological unrest. Jung responded by turning inward, recording visionary dialogues in his *Red Book* and building his Bollingen Tower as a retreat for inner work. Inayat Khan, meanwhile, brought Sufi teachings to the West, sensing a hunger for spiritual unity. Both saw that outer destruction demanded an inward renewal – an awakening to greater consciousness.

Apocalypse

Also today, we are living in a time of intersecting upheavals, where no single domain—geopolitical, ecological, social, or personal—can be viewed in isolation, and there is a widespread sense of something essential unraveling.

We can see with the naked eye how wars spill across borders, polarization corrodes trust, and ecological collapse severs our relationship with the living world.

Apocalyptic thinking, though often associated with annihilation, reminds us that what collapses today may not be only systems or structures but the very frameworks through which we make sense of reality — an apocalypse not of the world but of consciousness itself. This recalls a warning issued by philosopher Hannah Arendt.

In *The Origins of Totalitarianism*[1] (1951), Hannah Arendt identified loneliness and statelessness as the moral crises of modernity. Those who belong nowhere, she wrote, are stripped of the "right to have rights." Her warning resonates today, as rising nationalisms and declining protections bring this condition into renewed visibility.

DOI: 10.4324/9781003431336-9

Arendt also foresaw how truth itself might become expendable. In one of her most chilling insights, she wrote:

> The ideal subject of totalitarian rule is not the convinced Nazi or the convinced Communist, but people for whom the distinction between fact and fiction . . . and the distinction between true and false . . . no longer exist.[2]

What she described is beyond a political condition: it is a psychological one in the form of the dissolution of shared reality. Arendt's notion of a psychological dissolution of shared reality resonates today, as polarized media and misinformation erode our common sense of truth.

In parallel, technology intensifies the paradox of constant connection and growing isolation; algorithms anticipate desire while attention frays. The pandemic, for one, exposed how brittle our social fabric had already become. Journalist Mary McNamara illustrated it as a modern apocalypse where anxiety, anger, exhaustion, and dread replaced the Biblical Four Horsemen.

Where Did Consciousness Go Missing?

Consciousness has gone missing before — at the dusk of great civilizations when brilliance and exhaustion coincided, faltered from within from loss of coherence, trust, and vision The collective mind turned away from depth toward distraction, forgetting the inner ground on which it stood.

This forgetting resembles what Max Weber in 1917 called "the disenchantment of the world," when science and religion alike stripped life of depth. Disenchantment, in this sense, marks a narrowing of perception disconnected from the symbolic, the sacred, the imaginal.

Yet postwar enchantment never fully vanished but withdrew underground. Even those who embraced science, Freud,[3] among them, often turned privately to the irrational or occult practices. As Jason Josephson Storm argues in *The Myth of Disenchantment*,[4] the notion of a fully secular modernity is itself a myth. In reality, belief in magic, mysticism, and the unseen never truly disappeared.

Enchantment never truly vanished because it is not in the first place a stage of history but a mode of perception inseparable from consciousness itself. The impulse to experience the world as alive, meaningful, and responsive reasserts itself whenever imagination, symbol, or beauty restore participation between self and world.

The task today is to develop "consciousness." By this, I refer to opening ourselves to the processes that have been referenced in the works of both Jung and Inayat Khan. "Consciousness," in this sense, refers not simply to the waking state or to neural activity, but to the full awareness of reality. This psychological and spiritual development requires increasing the ego's capacity to experience the heights and depths of the world within and without. In Jung's understanding, it means expanding the ego's capacity to relate to and integrate the contents emerging from the total psyche, the Self. This is the individuation process, as described and exemplified by Jung.

Both Jung and Inayat Khan taught that consciousness evolves through relationship — with the unconscious, the divine, and the living world. Transformation, for each, is not an escape from the world but a deepening participation in it: for Jung, through creative dialogue with the unconscious; for Inayat Khan, through the attuned heart that perceives Love, Harmony, and Beauty within ordinary life.

What Is Consciousness?

To speak of consciousness is already to enter sacred territory. It lies at the heart of what it means to live, connecting us to ourselves, to others, and to the vast mystery of creation. Philosophers and scientists have sought to define it, yet consciousness remains an enigma, a living phenomenon that eludes reduction to simple formulas. At its highest levels, consciousness evokes awe, wonder, and love, transforming the mundane into the miraculous and opening new vistas of understanding and creativity. In short, consciousness is the movement of awareness — the living thread that unites all experience and the capacity of awareness to know itself.

The study of consciousness is as much an inquiry into the self as it is an exploration of the cosmos. It challenges us to move beyond asking how subjective experience emanates from matter, toward asking how consciousness can deepen, expand and develop. Higher states, where the boundaries of the ego grow permeable, reveal profound truths about the unity of being and remind us that consciousness is a dynamic field encompassing the fullest range of awareness.

Such breadth of awareness has long invited inquiry. Philosophers, neuroscientists, and mystics have offered diverse and sometimes conflicting perspectives, ranging from materialist explanations to deeply spiritual ones.

Among the more inwardly expansive perspectives are those of Carl Jung and Hazrat Inayat Khan. Jung did not take a view of consciousness as wakefulness or thought, but as the ego's capacity to relate to the unconscious in a continual process of integrating shadow, anima and animus, and Self. Inayat Khan, in turn, described consciousness as the mirror of the soul, reflecting aspects of the Divine into awareness. For both, consciousness is a creative and relational process through which the human being attunes to what is beyond the personal ego.

While Jung and Inayat Khan offer deeply psychological and spiritual frameworks for understanding consciousness, their insights are not isolated from broader currents of thought. Across physics, neuroscience, and philosophy, modern thinkers have likewise begun to challenge the materialist paradigm. David Bohm, Roger Penrose, and Dan Zahavi each suggest – in their own ways – that consciousness is more fundamental, participatory, and relational than traditionally assumed. Their ideas resonate with the inner dimensions explored in Carl Jung's psychology and Inayat Khan's mysticism. Let us briefly glance at how these three contemporary scholars engage in the discourse on the nature of consciousness.

Theoretical physicist David Bohm, with his concept of the "implicate order," challenges the reductionist view that consciousness arises solely from brain activity. Bohm proposes that the universe itself is participatory and fundamentally interconnected. What we perceive as discrete objects, events, and forms, belong to the *explicate order* - surface reality - while beneath it lies the *implicate order*: a hidden dimension where everything is enfolded into everything else. Here, separation is an illusion and reality is an *unbroken wholeness in movement*, as Bohm puts it.[5]

Like a hologram containing the whole image in every part, the implicate order contains the whole of reality in every point. Consciousness, in his view, is thus not confined to individual minds. Inayat Khan's teaching that the divine essence is hidden and revealed in all creation beautifully parallels Bohm's vision of unity.

Roger Penrose, Nobel Prize winning mathematician and anesthesiologist Stuart Hameroff,[6] proposed the Orchestrated Objective Reduction (Orch-OR)[7] theory which suggests that consciousness may arise from quantum processes within brain microtubules. These quantum events, they argue, are "orchestrated" by biological processes, and undergo "objective reduction" – a kind of quantum collapse that Penrose proposes to be linked to fundamental physical laws. Though highly debated and still speculative,[8] Orch-OR implies that consciousness may be an essential aspect of reality, not a byproduct of matter.

Philosopher Dan Zahavi offers yet another lens. His phenomenology views consciousness as a dynamic movement of lived experience rather than a static substance. In his concept of "inner time-consciousness"[9] perception and memory form a continuous temporal field that holds past, present, and future together. Our pre-reflective self-awareness, the immediate sense that our experiences are *ours,* reveals consciousness as implicitly self-aware, prior to reflection. For Zahavi, the self is not a fixed entity but a living center disclosed in the ongoing flow of experience.

What these contemporary thinkers share, despite their differing disciplines, is an effort to restore depth to the modern understanding of consciousness. Each, in his own way, undermines the assumption that consciousness is an isolated, secondary phenomenon. Bohm points to an underlying unity of being, Penrose to the possibility that consciousness is immanent in the universe itself, and Zahavi to its immediate presence within lived experience. Together, they gesture toward a view of consciousness not as mechanism but as mystery — a relational field in which matter, mind, and meaning participate. In this sense, their insights resonate with the vision of Jung and Inayat Khan, for whom consciousness is both the mirror and the medium of transformation.

Reaching Higher Consciousness

If we agree with reputable scholars[10] that there are signs the materialist dimension of consciousness — which has long informed the dominant paradigm of the modern West — is nearing exhaustion, we may also recognize that in this very decline lies the seed of renewal: the birth of new dimensions of consciousness with a different orientation toward the world and all its inhabitants.

Across both science and spirituality, evolution implies a movement toward greater complexity, awareness, and unity. In Sufi metaphysics, Ibn Arabi described existence as evolving through successive forms — from mineral to plant to animal to human — each stage of evolution carrying forward the essence of the previous one. Humanity, in his view, contains all prior dimensions within itself as living foundations for further refinement. In his vision, the Perfect Man gathers and makes conscious all levels of creation, uniting them in a being who mirrors the totality of existence.[11]

Existence itself follows an arc of descent and ascent, emanating from divine unity into multiplicity and returning again through the evolution of consciousness. Thus, consciousness does not evolve by transcending matter but by integrating it — awakening through the full spectrum of being.

In both Carl Jung and Inayat Khan, the next movement of consciousness is not elsewhere but otherwise — a quieter center, a heart attuned to unity, an imagination that reads symbols rather than clings to certainties. For Jung, this transformation happens as the ego becomes transparent to the Self through integration and creative dialogue with the unconscious.

Both taught that transformation occurs not by escaping the world but through fully, passionately participating in it. Sensory experience is therefore central to this journey.[12] To grasp such intangible states, sensory metaphors offer a vivid means of articulation. Taste, for instance, is an everyday experience capable of inducing ecstasy. Nowhere is this more vividly expressed than in the story of Rumi, whose entire inspiration is said to have been sparked by him eating a piece of sweet *halva* in Konya. Rumi's poetry overflows with allusions to food.[13] In Sufi poetry, *wine* serves as a powerful image of divine love. To drink the "wine of love" is to abandon the self, to dissolve into ecstatic absorption with the Beloved. Inayat Khan explained that love's wine, though intoxicating, ultimately brings clarity: If one succeeds in attaining this, one enjoys that union with the Beloved in a happy vision. This paradox – that intoxication leads to enlightenment – finds its psychological parallel in Jung's insight that one does not become enlightened by imagining figures of light, but by making the darkness within conscious.

Similarly, Jung's alchemical work is rich with sensory imagery: colors, tastes, shapes, and transformations. The "base" materials of life, when consciously engaged with, become the gold of spiritual realization.

At Bollingen, Jung carved alchemical and symbolic imagery, including Latin phrases. He later reflected that this act of carving gave form to something ineffable within himself. For him, it was a way of making the unconscious tangible. The tower itself became a living representation of his individuation process – a structure he physically built and expanded, laying bricks, shaping walls, and ensuring that each addition mirrored his own inner process. The act of carving was not a symbol of transformation – it was the transformation made manifest.

Higher consciousness is cultivated, not wished into being, in the crucible of life itself where joy and sorrow refine the spirit like fire tempers gold. Jung's practices of active imagination, dream work, and symbolic engagement train the psyche to converse across body, mind, and soul. Inayat Khan's disciplines of prayer, breath, *wazifa*, and *zikr* refine receptivity and remembrance attuning the heart to Love, Harmony, and Beauty, perceiving the divine pattern within ordinary life. Equally central to this evolution are peace and joy, which come to light when the heart opens to love in its most expansive sense. *Joy* is the desire of attainment by the world; *peace* is the attainment of heaven. Both paths are disciplined arts of attention — the essence of individuation and self-realization — through which perception is purified and life is read more truly.

What unites these paths is guidance — the felt emergence of meaning that cannot be forced. In psychoanalysis, guidance constellates in the field between analyst and analysand; in the Sufi path, between *murshid* and *mureed* — and inwardly, as the subtle directive of the heart.

The Guide Within

The figure of Khidr — the mysterious initiator of Moses — names this inner companion, the friend of the soul who teaches through unknowing and leads beyond the small ego's map. Jung spoke of the "colloquy with the friend of the soul," emphasizing the necessity of inner dialogue with a guiding presence. In this context, Khidr symbolizes the emergence of higher consciousness and the journey toward wholeness. Jung recounts a dream in which a treasure lies hidden in the sea. To reach it, he must dive through a narrow, perilous opening into the depths. In the depths below he finds a friend, the friend he had longed for all his life. Jung realized that the true treasure was the companion himself.

In Sufi tradition, Khidr's first lesson to Moses was deceptively simple: "Do not speak." Inayat Khan recounts the story of Moses walking through the beauty of nature with Khidr, who was preparing him for prophetship. The teacher was absorbed in divine presence, and Moses felt it deeply; yet as their journey continued, he repeatedly failed to withhold judgment over Khidr's bewildering actions — acts whose meaning only later became clear.

The story mirrors the inner path itself: it teaches humility before the unknown and trust in a wisdom that moves beneath reason. Khidr is the companion who leads us through unknowing, inviting surrender into the living current of truth.

As Inayat Khan reminds us:

The man who realizes God as a friend is never lonely in the world, neither in this world nor in the hereafter. There is always a friend, a friend in the crowd, a friend in the solitude; or while he is asleep, unconscious of this outer world, and when he is awake and conscious of it. In both cases the friend is there in his thought, in his imagination, in his heart, in his soul.[14]

The fruit of this journey is embodied freedom, not an escape from the human condition but its transfiguration. In Jungian terms, the Self lives consciously through one's words, hands, and choices; in Sufi terms, *baqa* — abiding — dawns after the false self loosens its grip. Body, mind, heart, and soul move in one rhythm. Heaven and earth are no longer two.

Jung, in *Answer to Job*, proposed that what humanity brings to God is consciousness — the human capacity to reflect, to suffer, and to know. Through individuation, the divine becomes more conscious in and through the human soul.

This vision finds deep resonance in Hazrat Inayat Khan's teaching on the stages of knowledge. In the stage of *Haqiqat*, one awakens to a deeper truth: that God has been seeing through our eyes, hearing through our ears, breathing through our breath. What once seemed to be our own body is now revealed as the living temple of God.

No longer seeking the divine as distant, one realizes it has always been within. In both perspectives, higher consciousness brings personal fulfillment — and participates in the divine's own self-realization.

Thus ultimately, the journey of individuation and self-realization is the awakening of God to God through the human heart: the quiet union where being and knowing become one.

In such awakening, the task of our time is renewed: to live as witnesses of that unity in a world still learning to remember it.

Notes

1 Hannah Arendt, *The Origins of Totalitarianism* (New York: Harcourt, Brace, 1951), 376–377.
2 Hannah Arendt, *The Origins of Totalitarianism* (New York: Harcourt, Brace, 1951), 474.
3 Freud participated in table-turning sessions (a form of séance or spiritualist communication) with members of his inner circle, including Sandor Ferenczi. While he maintained a skeptical stance, he was privately intrigued.
4 Jason Ānanda Josephson Storm, *The Myth of Disenchantment: Magic, Modernity, and the Birth of the Human Sciences* (Chicago: University of Chicago Press, 2017).
5 Bohm, David. *Wholeness and the Implicate Order*. London: Routledge, 1980. And general Bohm, David. *On Dialogue*. Edited by Lee Nichol. London: Routledge, 1996.
6 Hameroff, Stuart, and Roger Penrose. "Consciousness in the Universe: A Review of the 'Orch OR' Theory." *Physics of Life Reviews* 11, no. 1 (March 2014): 39–78.
7 See, for example, "Consciousness in the Universe: A Review of the 'Orch OR' Theory" (*Physics of Life Reviews*, 2014.
8 Koch, Christof. *The Feeling of Life Itself: Why Consciousness Is Widespread but Can't Be Computed*. Cambridge, MA: MIT Press, 2019. Christof Koch argues that the Orch-OR theory is highly speculative and lacks experimental support, particularly regarding the role of quantum coherence in the brain's warm, wet biological environment — which, he suggests, is too noisy for delicate quantum processes to be sustained. He also questions whether microtubules play any central role in neural computation, emphasizing that current neuroscience finds no need to invoke quantum mechanisms to explain consciousness.
9 Dan Zahavi, "Inner Time-Consciousness and Pre-Reflective Self-Awareness." In *The Phenomenological Mind*, ed. Shaun Gallagher and Dan Zahavi (London: Routledge,

2005), 200–214. And, general, Dan Zahavi, *Phenomenology: The Basics* (London: Routledge, 2019).

10   Iain McGilchrist, *The Matter with Things: Our Brains, Our Delusions, and the Unmaking of the World* (London: Perspectiva Press, 2021); Andreas Weber, *Enlivenment: Toward a Poetics for the Anthropocene* (Cambridge, MA: MIT Press, 2019); and Evan Thompson, *Mind in Life: Biology, Phenomenology, and the Sciences of Mind* (Cambridge, MA: Harvard University Press, 2007). Each argues, in distinct ways, that the materialist paradigm underlying modern Western thought and its understanding of consciousness is reaching its conceptual limits, and that a more relational, integrative view of consciousness and reality is emerging.

11   William C. Chittick, *The Sufi Path of Knowledge: Ibn al-ʿArabi's Metaphysics of Imagination* (Albany: State University of New York Press, 1989), 379–381. Chittick explains that "Man brings together all the levels of existence, from the most spiritual to the most corporeal. Hence he is the locus of manifestation for the totality of the Divine Names." See also Henry Corbin, *Creative Imagination in the Sufism of Ibn Arabi*, trans. Ralph Manheim (Princeton: Princeton University Press, 1969), 85, where Corbin describes the Perfect Man as "the eye through which God contemplates Himself in His theophanies."

12   In contrast, an influential modern example of *sensory deprivation* used for inner exploration is the floatation tank, developed in the 1950s by neuroscientist John C. Lilly. Enclosed in darkness, soundlessness, and buoyed in body-temperature salt water, the individual is cut off from all sensory input, facilitating altered states of consciousness. Lilly associated these states with deep layers of the psyche and even mystical insight. While such practices align with ascetic traditions that emphasize withdrawal from the senses, my approach emphasizes the *refinement* rather than the *suspension* of sensory experience as a pathway toward deeper spiritual awareness, individuation and self-realization. See John C. Lilly, *The Deep Self: Consciousness Exploration in the Isolation Tank* (New York: Simon & Schuster, 1977).

13   A. M. Schimmel, *Deciphering the Signs of God: A Phenomenological Approach to Islam* (State University of New York Press, 1994), 107.

14   Hazrat Inayat Khan, *The Supplementary Papers: Metaphysics 4, Unity*. Unpublished paper. Author's collection.

Chapter 10

Epilogue

There comes a point in any deep inquiry when the material turns back on the one who set it in motion. Writing this book has been a process of immersion – into Jung's symbolic language, Inayat Khan's mystical vision, and the bridge between them. It has been, at times, a disciplined effort, a pursuit of clarity, but at other times, a kind of surrender, allowing meaning to surface in its own time. I have often found myself wondering: "Was I writing this book, or was the book writing me?"

Stepping into the inner worlds of Jung and Inayat Khan has inevitably shaped my own experience. Their ideas are not merely subjects of study; they have become living presences, influencing the contours of thought and perception. Eminent scholars and close companions of both men have already produced thorough and reliable biographies, offering detailed accounts of their lives and work. The challenge, then, was not in retelling what was already known, but in navigating the fine line between scholarship and lived experience.

Yet how else could I make comparisons without revealing what was being compared? The task demanded more than analysis – it required participation. It is my hope that the sensitive reader may, at times, experience moments of proximity with Jung and Inayat Khan through my personal familiarity with each of them. Perhaps as a moment of recognition, or, perhaps as a moment of disbelief.

If I had to name what this journey has given me, it would be a finer attunement to the subtle, the in-between, the connective tissue of experience that holds intellect and soul, reason and imagination, self and world together. The very questions I have posed – about individuation, self-realization, consciousness – have demanded that I live them, not simply analyze them. Writing about Jung, I encountered my own inner figures more sharply. Writing about Inayat Khan, I became more aware of the rhythm of my own breath, the resonance of silence.

Following Jung into his world of dreams, visions, imagination, and direct encounters with the unconscious – his *Red Book* – required effort. The deeper he went, the more I had to follow, as a scholar and as a participant. My mind "writes" mainly in the early morning, when the world is still, before thought and movement disturb the quiet. In that pre-dawn space, there were moments when I heard his voice – explaining, elaborating, offering new associations and references to the ideas I was working on. And before waking fully, at times around 4 a.m., I would

DOI: 10.4324/9781003431336-10

find myself caught in tremendous dreams – whirls of visions, impressions, and emotions. They were not always coherent to me, but they were unmistakably Jungian in nature. His presence in my work was not a distant one; it was immersive.

Jung's directive, "You must differentiate," echoed in my mind. But differentiation, as I quickly learned, was not always easy. At times, I felt like someone clinging to a tiny piece of wood in a stormy sea, trying to discern patterns in the chaos. Eventually, I learned to ask within the dream itself: "What do you mean by X, Y, Z?" Or I'd find myself sighing with self-pity, saying: "Here I am busy integrating all my opposites, and now you tell me to differentiate!" – a quiet inquiry that sometimes yielded unexpected clarity.

With Inayat Khan, the challenge took on a different form. Having studied his teachings for decades – my Ph.D., after all, was on his Sufism – I knew his words too well. I would come to key passages, essential to self-realization, and feel an inner sigh: *Not again. I know this already.* A weight settled in, accompanied by the critical voice: "You are not saying anything new. Besides, there are already volumes out there saying the same thing." My task here was not to analyze further but to unlearn – to forget what I thought I knew, to create space for seeing anew.

Every morning, before I begin the actual writing, I start by journaling anything that stood out from a dream or an idea. But rather than simply setting it aside, I engage in the practice of Active Imagination – a technique I was taught by my Jungian supervisor, Murray Stein, whose insight and guidance over more than 20 years in Zurich have been invaluable to my work. Then I do the Sufi practices I have been taught: a short prayer, a breathing exercise, sometimes a *wazifa* or a brief *zikr*, followed by stillness and silence. The latter is what matters most to me, though the preceding practices pave the way for it. That silence is not only an absence of sound or movement; it is the stillness of body, mind, heart, and soul – a suspension of thought, a silence that is lived rather than enforced. In that space, I do not move, think, or strive to feel. The experience of consciousness, free from content, is peace.

Yet, even in that silence, something stirs: a drop of awareness, a glimpse of a larger truth, a quiet correction in an invisible matrix. And suddenly, in that moment of clarity, I find myself drawn back – revising once more, ready to take the work one step further.

More than anything, I have come to see this work not as an academic pursuit, nor even as a personal quest, but as part of something larger – an ongoing movement of consciousness seeking to know itself. Jung spoke of individuation as a necessity, an instinct embedded in the psyche. Inayat Khan spoke of self-realization as the soul's longing to return to its source. To me, they are not separate. The path to wholeness is at once deeply personal and profoundly universal.

Individuation, shaped through the guidance, supervision, and analysis I have received, and self-realization, nurtured through my Sufi training, have essentially been the irrefutable return to my sense of being – something fundamental, something always present. Though I speak of these processes as journeys – and they certainly are – it would be a mistake to envision them as a cumulative ascent, a gradual augmentation of the psyche and soul. In truth, the stillness and silence I just described are not new experiences to me. I recall them as vividly in the quiet of my present life as I did as a child playing alone, drawing circles in the sand, or even in the ineffable awareness of being a fetus in the womb. My sense of being has remained unchanged. There is nothing I could do – nothing I *would* do – to alter that fundamental presence.

What individuation and self-realization have provided are indispensable pathways through the jungle of life's demands, wounds, and the weight of others' expectations. They have been the means by which I have learned to safeguard the only thing that is truly mine – the one thing I cannot avoid – *me.*

This book was written with the reader in mind, but also with the awareness that books, like seeds, fall into different kinds of soil. Some will take root immediately; others may lie dormant until the conditions are right. What I hope is that, in some way, this work has opened a space – for reflection, for recognition, for an inward listening that is too often drowned out by the noise of the world.

My lifelong engagement with psychology and spirituality has naturally shaped my choices – in academia, in my career, in my relationships, in my way of life, and even in how I raised my children. It may seem counterintuitive that, for most of my professional life, I have worked with senior executives of large corporations. After all, one might not expect a psychoanalyst – and a Sufi, no less – to be drawn to the world of business leadership. The reason for this assumption lies in a pervasive modern myth: that those who have worked tirelessly to attain and sustain positions of power must be oblivious to self-reflection. CEOs are often, ironically not seldom in "mindfulness" circles, cast as the other – as nothing but hardheaded decision-makers, devoid of introspection. William James, in his *Pragmatism*, speaks of the "nothing-but" fallacy: "What is higher, is explained by what is lower and treated for ever as a case of 'nothing but' – nothing but something else of an inferior sort." One could see such a view as a psychological compensation – a way to simplify complexity by reducing individuals to mere functions.

Yet my own experience has been quite different. In working with leaders across industries and continents, I have not found them to be superficial or uninterested in their inner lives. If anything, the common thread that unites them is a hunger for insight – a readiness to grasp it with both hands and explore what it means for their work, their decisions, and their personal development. In my work with women's personal development groups – held in different cultural contexts with the intention of integrating awareness from the start – I have seen how such spaces foster personal realization and a felt sense of how consciousness expands through relatedness. Beyond individual growth, this work is part of a larger cultural shift – a movement toward a global consciousness that values connection over hierarchy, inclusion over separation. The women who engage in this process develop a deeper awareness of why it matters *how we are* with one another – respectful, patient, open, both serious and humorous. In doing so, they embody a leadership model that centers shared humanity, one that contrasts with traditional hierarchical structures. This experience does not stay within the group; it moves with them, shaping how they lead, influence, and contribute to a collective transformation once they return home.

Another trait shared by executives who I have worked with is *curiosity*. This, of course, is a trait that serves them well in their professional sphere, where success often depends on an ability to anticipate change, seek new perspectives, and remain adaptable. But what happens when that same curiosity is turned inward? What happens when they are invited to step beyond their familiar frameworks – to peer over the fence, to look beneath the surface, to search the attic, so to speak?

This is precisely where my background as both a psychoanalyst and a Sufi becomes essential. The work I do is built on the very pillars of individuation and self-realization that I have explored in this book. It is an invitation – to pause, to experience the presence of another who listens deeply, who reflects back, sometimes through a question but often in silence. When that *vibe* – consciousness speaking to consciousness – becomes active, something shifts. The whole room comes alive. In that moment, true exploration begins. And that is when I know I am truly effective in my profession.

As for myself, I leave this work with a deepened sense of trust. That consciousness is not something we build, but something we return to. That the real work is not in constructing a theory, but in learning to live what we know. And that the call of consciousness, in the end, is never abstract. It is intimate, precise, alive.

And so, having followed this thread to its end, I find that it does not end at all. The conversation continues.

Bibliography

Burston, Daniel. 2021. *Anti-Semitism and Analytical Psychology: Jung, Politics and Culture*. Routledge.

Chittick, William C. 1989. *The Sufi Path of Knowledge: Ibn al-'Arabi's Metaphysics of Imagination*. State University of New York Press.

Clay, Catrine. 2016. *Labyrinths: Emma Jung, Her Marriage to Carl, and the Early Years of Psychoanalysis*. HarperCollins.

Corbin, Henry. 1969. *Alone with the Alone: Creative Imagination in the Sufism of Ibn 'Arabi*. Bollingen Series XCI:7, trans. Ralph Manheim (Princeton, NJ: Princeton University Press).

Freedman, Ralph. 1996. *Life of a Poet: Rainer Maria Rilke*. Northwestern University Press.

Freud, Sigmund, and Carl Gustav Jung. 1974. *The Freud-Jung Letters: The Correspondence Between Sigmund Freud and CG Jung*. William McGuire. Princeton University Press.

Gadamer, Hans-Georg. 1989. *Truth and Method, Tr. Joel Weinsheimer and Donald G. Marshall*. Crossroad.

Hameroff, Stuart, and Roger Penrose. "Consciousness in the Universe: A Review of the 'Orch OR' Theory." *Physics of Life Reviews* 11, no. 1 (March 2014): 39–78.

Heidegger, Martin, John Macquarrie, and Edward Robinson. 1962. *Being and Time*. Blackwell.

Hofstede, Geert, Gert Jan Hofstede, and Michael Minkov. 2010. *Cultures and Organizations: Intercultural Cooperation and Its Importance for Survival*. 3rd ed. McGraw-Hill.

Hood, Ralph W. 1976. "Conceptual Criticisms of Regressive Explanations of Mysticism." *Review of Religious Research* 17, no. 3: 179.

Husserl, Edmund. 1989. *Ideas Pertaining to a Pure Phenomenology and to a Phenomenological Philosophy: Second Book Studies in the Phenomenology of Constitution*. 3 vols. Springer Science & Business Media.

Jaffé, Aniela. 2023. *Reflections on the Life and Dreams of C.G. Jung*. Translated by Caitlin Stephens, with Commentary by Elena Fischli. Daimon Verlag.

James, William. 2002. *The Varieties of Religious Experience*. Modern Library.

Jironet, Karin. 2002. *The Image of Spiritual Liberty in the Sufi Movement Following Hazrat Inayat Khan*. Leuven: Peeters Publishers.

Jironet, Karin. 2009. *Sufi Mysticism into the West: Life and Leadership of Hazrat Inayat Khan's Brothers 1927–1967 (New Religious Identities in the Western World)*. Leuven: Peeters Publishers.

Josephson-Storm, Jason A. 2017. *The Myth of Disenchantment: Magic, Modernity, and the Birth of the Human Sciences*. University of Chicago Press.

Jung, Carl G. 1951. *Aion: Researches into the Phenomenology of the Self. The Collected Works of C. G. Jung*. 9ii vols. Princeton University Press.

Jung, Carl G. 1959. *The Archetypes and the Collective Unconscious. The Collected Works of C.G. Jung*. 9i vols. Princeton University Press.

Jung, Carl G. 1963. *Mysterium Coniunctionis: An Inquiry into the Separation and Synthesis of Psychic Opposites in Alchemy*. Princeton University Press.

Jung, Carl G. 1968. *Psychology and Alchemy. The Collected Works of C.G. Jung*. 12 vols. Princeton University Press.

Jung, Carl G. 1969. *The Structure and Dynamics of the Psyche. The Collected Works of C.G. Jung*. 8 vols. Princeton University Press.

Jung, Carl G. 1971. *Psychological Types. The Collected Works of C.G. Jung*. 6 vols. Princeton University Press.

Jung, Carl G. 1974. *C.G. Jung Letters Vol. II*. 2 vols. Princeton University Press.

Jung, Carl G. 1989. *Memories, Dreams, Reflections*. Vol. 268. Vintage.

Jung, C. G. 1989. *Letters*. Vol. 2. Princeton University Press.

Jung, Carl G., Sonu Ed Shamdasani, Mark Trans Kyburz, and John Trans Peck. 2009. *The Red Book: Liber Novus*. W. W. Norton & Co.

Jung, Carl G., Sonu Shamdasani, Martin Liebscher, and John Peck. 2020. *The Black Books: 1913–1932: Notebooks of Transformation*. W. W. Norton & Company.

Jung, Emma. 1986. *The Grail Legend*. Translated by Andrea Dykes, with Marie-Louise von Franz. Princeton University Press.

Karin Jironet, *The Image of Spiritual Liberty in the Sufi Movement Following Hazrat Inayat Khan* (Leuven: Peeters Publishers, 2002).

Khan, Hazrat Inayat. 1988a. *A Sufi Message of Spiritual Liberty, Ecstasy, Male and Female Aspects of God. Vol. The Sufi Message*. 5 vols. Motilal Banarsidass.

Khan, Hazrat Inayat. 1988b. *Gathas: Everyday Life. Vol. The Sufi Message*. 13 vols. Motilal Banarsidass.

Khan, Hazrat Inayat. 1988c. *In an Eastern Rose Garden: The Master Mind. Vol. The Sufi Message*. 7 vols. Motilal Banarsidass.

Khan, Hazrat Inayat. 1988d. *Metaphysics: The Experience of the Soul in Different Planes of Existence. Vol. The Sufi Message*. 5 vols. Motilal Banarsidass.

Khan, Hazrat Inayat. 1988e. *Nasihat, Advice: Relation to the Teachers. Vol. The Sufi Message*. 1 vols. Motilal Banarsidass.

Khan, Hazrat Inayat. 1988f. *The Mysticism of Sound and Music. Vol. The Sufi Message*. 2 vols. Motilal Banarsidass.

Khan, Hazrat Inayat. 1988g. *The Power of the Word. Vol. The Sufi Message*. 2 vols. Motilal Banarsidass.

Khan, Hazrat Inayat. 1988h. *The Soul, Whence and Whither? Vol. The Sufi Message*. 1 vols. Motilal Banarsidass.

Khan, Hazrat Inayat. 1988i. *The Spirit in the Flesh. Vol. The Healing Papers*. 2 vols. Motilal Banarsidass.

Khan, Hazrat Inayat. 1988j. *The Unity of Religious Ideals: The Spiritual Hierarchy, Government. Vol. The Sufi Message*. 9 vols. Motilal Banarsidass.

Khan, Hazrat Inayat. n.d. *Mysticism 2, About the Five Planes. Vol. The Supplementary Papers*. 1 vols. Motilal Banarsidass.

Koch, Christof. 2019. *The Feeling of Life Itself: Why Consciousness Is Widespread But Can't Be Computed*. MIT Press.

Lilly, John C. 1977. *The Deep Self: Consciousness Exploration in the Isolation Tank*. Simon & Schuster.

McGilchrist. Iain. 2021. *The Matter with Things: Our Brains, Our Delusions, and the Unmaking of the World*. Perspectiva Press.

Merleau-Ponty, Maurice. 2012. *Phenomenology of Perception*. Translated by Donald A. Landes. Routledge.

Nietzsche, Friedrich. 1984. *Human, All Too Human: A Book for Free Spirits*. Translated by Marion Faber and Stephen Lehmann. University of Nebraska Press.

Rilke, Rainer Maria. 1941. *The Book of Pilgrimage. Vol. 2 of the Book of Hours*. Translated by Babette Deutsch. New Directions Publishing.

Rudolf, Otto. 1958. *The Idea of the Holy*. Oxford University Press.

Schoenl, William J. 1998. *CG Jung: His Friendships with Mary Mellon and JB Priestley*. Chiron Publications.

Schimmel A. M. 1994. *Deciphering the Signs of God: A Phenomenological Approach to Islam*, 107. State University of New York Press.

Stace, Walter T. 1960. *Mysticism and Philosophy*. 1960th ed. Macmillan.

Stam, Kismet Dorothea. *Diary, 1923–1926*. Unpublished manuscript.

Thompson, Evan. 2007. *Mind in Life: Biology, Phenomenology, and the Sciences of Mind*. Harvard University Press.

Tolstoy, Leo. 1884. *My Confession*.

Tolstoy, Leo. 1894. *The Kingdom of God Is Within You*. Trans. Constance Garnett. Cassell Publishing Co.

Van Lommel, Pim. 2011. *Consciousness Beyond Life: The Science of the Near-Death Experience*. Harper Collins.

Van Tuyll van Serooskerken, Saida. Unpublished. *Memories of Pir-O-Murshid*. Private Collection. Part of the Smith Kerbert Collection, nr. 90, Archived at the Nekbakht Foundation, Suresnes, France.

von Franz, Marie-Louise. 1977. *Alchemical Active Imagination*. Shambhala.

von Franz, Marie-Louise. 1957. *Aurora Consurgens: A Document Attributed to Thomas Aquinas on the Problem of Opposites in Alchemy*. C. G. Jung Institute.

von Franz, Marie-Louise. 2006. *Corpus Alchemicum Arabicum*. Living Human Heritage Publications.

Weber, Andreas. 2019. *Enlivenment: Toward a Poetics for the Anthropocene*. MIT Press.

Wilhelm, Richard, trans. 1931. *The Secret of the Golden Flower: A Chinese Book of Life*. With a Foreword and Commentary by C. G. Jung. Routledge & Kegan Paul.

Zahavi, Dan. "Inner Time-Consciousness and Pre-Reflective Self-Awareness." In *The Phenomenological Mind*, edited by Shaun Gallagher and Dan Zahavi, 200–214. Routledge.

Zahavi, Dan. 2008. *Subjectivity and Selfhood: Investigating the First-Person Perspective*. MIT Press.

Index

For Product Safety Concerns and Information please contact our EU
representative GPSR@taylorandfrancis.com
Taylor & Francis Verlag GmbH, Kaufingerstraße 24, 80331 München, Germany